Come, Let Us Sing to the Lord

Wycliffe Studies in Gospel, Church, and Culture

This series, emanating from Wycliffe College, Toronto, addresses key topics and issues in the church and in contemporary culture.

Grounded in the historic tradition of the Christian faith, the series presents topical subject matter in an accessible form and seeks to appeal to a broad audience.

Typically titles in the series derive from sermons given by the faculty of Wycliffe College, Toronto, in its Founders' Chapel. The current volume on the Songs of Scripture is the third in the series and derives from a sermon series given in the Fall of 2016.

Come, Let Us Sing to the Lord

Songs of Scripture

EDITED BY
Katherine Kennedy Steiner

WIPF & STOCK · Eugene, Oregon

COME, LET US SING TO THE LORD
Songs of Scripture

Wycliffe Studies in Gospel, Church, and Culture

Copyright © 2017 Katherine Kennedy Steiner. All rights reserved. Except for brief quotations in critical publications or reviews, no part of this book may be reproduced in any manner without prior written permission from the publisher. Write: Permissions, Wipf and Stock Publishers, 199 W. 8th Ave., Suite 3, Eugene, OR 97401.

Wipf & Stock
An Imprint of Wipf and Stock Publishers
199 W. 8th Ave., Suite 3
Eugene, OR 97401

www.wipfandstock.com

PAPERBACK ISBN: 978-1-5326-3301-0
HARDCOVER ISBN: 978-1-5326-3303-4
EBOOK ISBN: 978-1-5326-3302-7

The English translations of the *Magnificat* (Luke 1:46-55) and the *Sanctus* (Is. 6:3 and Matt. 21:9) were prepared by the International Consultation on English Texts (ICET), 1975.

The English translation of the *Song of Moses* is excerpted from The Book of Alternative Services for the Anglican Church of Canada (Anglican Book Centre, Toronto). Copyright 1985 by the General Synod of the Anglican Church in Canada. Used with permission.

The English translations of the *Venite, exultemus* (Psalm 95), the *Benedicite Omnia Opera* (Daniel 3), the *Benedictus* (Luke 1:68-79), and the *Dignus es* (Rev 4:11; 5:9–10, 13) are excerpted from The Book Of Common Prayer and Administration of the Sacraments and Other Rites and Ceremonies of the Church: Together with the Psalter or Psalms of David According to the Use of the Episcopal Church. (New York:Seabury Press, 1979).

Scripture quotations marked ESV are from The ESV® Bible (The Holy Bible, English Standard Version®), copyright © 2001 by Crossway, a publishing ministry of Good News Publishers. Used by permission. All rights reserved.

Scripture quotations marked MSG are taken from *THE MESSAGE*, copyright © 1993, 1994, 1995, 1996, 2000, 2001, 2002 by Eugene H. Peterson. Used by permission of NavPress. All rights reserved. Represented by Tyndale House Publishers, Inc.

Scripture quotations marked NRSV are taken from New Revised Standard Version Bible, copyright © 1989 National Council of the Churches of Christ in the United States of America. Used by permission. All rights reserved worldwide.

Manufactured in the U.S.A.

Contents

Abbreviations | ix

Introduction: The Songs We Sing | xi
 —Katherine Kennedy Steiner

1 Being God's Song: *Venite, exultemus Domino* | 1
 —Ephraim Radner

2 Song of Deliverance: *Cantemus Domino* | 9
 —Peter Robinson

3 Of God's Victory: The Song of Deborah | 15
 —Marion Taylor

4 All Creation Sings: *Benedicite Omnia Opera* | 27
 —Thomas P. Power

5 A Lament: How the Mighty Have Fallen | 34
 —Annette Brownlee

6 Fearless Heralds: The Song of Good News | 40
 —J. Glen Taylor

Contents

7 The Dawn of Salvation: *Benedictus* | 45
   —Stephen G. W. Andrews

8 Mary's Victorious Child: *Magnificat* | 53
   —Terry Donaldson

9 Waiting for Salvation: *Nunc Dimittis* | 60
   —Alan L. Hayes

10 Being Like Christ: A Hymn to Christ | 65
    —L. Ann Jervis

11 A Holy God: *Sanctus* | 72
    —Judy Paulsen

12 Sing, Church: *Dignus es* | 77
    —Joseph L. Mangina

Bibliography | 85

List of Contributors | 87

Abbreviations

BAS   *Book of Alternative Services*, Anglican Church of Canada

BCP   *Book of Common Prayer*, Anglican Church of Canada

BCP1979   *Book of Common Prayer*, The Episcopal Church

PL   *Patrologia Latina*, edited by J. P. Migne

Introduction:
The Songs We Sing

Katherine Kennedy Steiner

The canticles, the songs in Scripture sung by the church, are the language of worship. Along with the book of Psalms they have offered Christians words with which to voice our praise and thanksgiving, ours joys and our laments. The meditations offered in this book examine what those songs say about us and our God.

Many of these meditations also consider the act of singing itself as our offering of worship. Why is it important that we *sing* our praise of God, not simply speak it? Some songs themselves even begin by enjoining us to sing: "I will sing to the Lord" (Song of Moses and Miriam), "Come, let us sing to the Lord" (Psalm 95). Singing God's praise is essential to who we are as the people of God. God made us to sing.

This is why from the early period Christians used the psalms and canticles to shape their daily prayers, Eucharistic liturgies, and liturgical calendars. Morning, evening, and night, Christians have used songs of Scripture to praise God, who is the creator of the day and night. The Song of

Introduction: The Songs We Sing

Zechariah, sung in the morning office in the Anglican tradition, orients us to the dawning sun that reflects Christ, our true light. The Song of Simeon reminds us at the close of the day that we, having witnessed Christ's salvation, need not fear death. The Song of Moses and Miriam, traditionally sung at Easter, gives us a song of liberation, showing us how we are like the Israelites whose foe was drowned in the Red Sea.

The songs in Scripture that have been sung in the liturgy in the Western church have been given their Latin names, as they are still frequently referred to in the worship life of the church. But we have also included in this compilation a few biblical songs that the church has not found a lasting home for in the liturgy, although each of them was certainly sung at various points in history. The Philippians hymn is perhaps the oldest known Christian hymn, and has inspired countless new hymns, but has not regularly been sung in its original form. The Song of Deborah and the Lament of David were both briefly popular as metrical hymns in the reformed early American church.

In every age of the church, Christian communities have found different ways of singing these songs together, but their musical concerns have been similar. What music honors the biblical text? Is a literal or poetic translation of the text more appropriate for congregational song? What musical setting helps us sing our praise together? What musical setting best displays the gift of song God has given us?

Perhaps not surprisingly, Christians have answered these questions differently. We know as little about how the songs of Scripture might have been sung by Jews during Jesus' life on earth as we do about how Christians in the early church sang them. Perhaps that lack of knowledge is a

Introduction: The Songs We Sing

blessing, because it has freed us from any illusions that we could stick to biblical music. Instead, in every age Christians asked how best to sing these songs to God together. Saint Augustine (354–430) expressed well in his *Confessions* the tension that Christians have felt about what kind of music should be used for singing the Psalms. He wrote compellingly in Book 10 of the *Confessions* of how the "delight of the ear" drew him into worship, but he worried that he loved the song more than the words that give the song life. Recalling what he had heard of the practice in Alexandria, he concluded that recitation that was closer to speaking than singing seemed safer. Yet he saw the benefit of congregational singing, despite the temptation to love the song more than the God who gave it. In Epistle 55, speaking of singing the biblical songs, he concluded that there is nothing better, nothing more beneficial, nothing more holy than Christians singing together.

So we sing the songs examined in this book because they are the songs of praise that belong to the whole church. From sung speech to the most jubilant song, we blend our voices into one people whom God has called together, each one by name.

The most basic method of singing the biblical texts common to both Eastern and Western Christians, and one we frequently use at Wycliffe Chapel, is plainchant—simple recitation sung antiphonally, that is, back and forth between two groups. In simple recitation most of the verse is sung on one pitch, but the half verse and whole verse are marked by cadences—a short one at the half verse, and a longer cadence at the whole verse. The very earliest music notation that survives in the West is in ninth-century manuals for cantors, which provide eight different tones on which to sing the biblical songs, corresponding to eight musical modes. These eight modes were inherited from the ancient Greeks (although they were misunderstood in the West) and were believed to govern or order all music. The tones based on those modes were designed to reflect the various natures of each of the eight modes. In other words, the earliest musical evidence we have in the West indicates that Christians sang the biblical songs using slightly elaborated recitation, respecting primarily the grammar of the text, to a set of tones that covered every inch of what they understood as music.

In contrast, current Western music theory considers the half step the normative means of organizing sound, and lots of new art music seeks to use every half step in one piece. Almost all of our hymns, on the other hand, are in just two scales, major and minor, which developed from two of the eight pre-modern modes. This is part of the reason it sounds odd, archaic, and sometimes rather somber when we sing the psalms and canticles to the ancient tones. But when we sing using these pre-modern tones, we are using melodies that pre-modern Christians believed governed the entirety of God's created world of music, gathering up all of creation in our offering of praise and thanksgiving.

As choirs got more and more sophisticated over the medieval period, and took over the majority of the singing in worship, they also developed ways of embellishing the chanting. Since recitation was so straightforward (and every good chorister had the psalms and canticles memorized), harmony could easily be improvised around it. The most famous example of this kind of improvised harmony is the *Miserere mei*, Psalm 51, by Gregorio Allegri (1582–1652), often sung on Ash Wednesday in churches with strong choirs. By the seventeenth century these harmonized recited psalms had taken on a life of their own in

Introduction: The Songs We Sing

the best choirs in England, particularly in royal chapels and major cathedrals. Choir masters started writing their own psalm chants, not necessarily based on the eight Latin tones from the medieval period. We now refer to these Anglican chants by the name of the composer.

This harmonically complex method of singing the psalms and canticles was primarily practiced in larger cathedral choirs until the nineteenth century, when smaller parishes were interested in replicating the beauty of cathedral worship. So Anglican chant became a more normalized and accessible practice, witnessed by the fact that there are several Anglican chant settings of psalms and canticles in Anglican hymnals such as *Common Praise*, the standard hymnal for the Anglican Church of Canada. In the ideal form, Anglican chant is sung by opposing choirs in four strong parts, but it is still beautiful when only the top line is sung and the organ accompanies (for great choral examples, search King's College Cambridge or St. John's College Cambridge and Anglican chant on youtube.com).

With the Reformation and the interest in translating the Bible into the vernacular came a new form of singing Scripture: metrical hymns. The Vulgate, the Latin translation of the Bible used in the West since St. Jerome (d. 420) that translated the Psalms from the Greek Septuagint, did not attempt to impose any poetic structure, except to maintain the division at the half verse. But as the songs were translated into English and other vernacular languages, translators sought out ways of creating poetic versions that would mimic the vernacular poetry of hymnody.

One early English example of metrical psalms with a collection of melodies was published in 1567, compiled by the Archbishop of Canterbury, Matthew Parker. It contains metrical translations of the entire Psalter with summaries of the "argument" of each psalm, and a collect at the end. It also includes metrical versions of the canticles for morning and evening prayer. At the end, the book includes eight tunes in four parts, suggesting that the tunes can be used for any of the metrical psalms or canticles. The eight tunes are hymn-like settings written by Thomas Tallis, although a bit complicated for the average congregation. An example is his "Why fumeth in sight," the tune of which is still used in hymnals today, including *Common Praise*. The introduction suggests that they be sung or played privately as a domestic form of sacred entertainment. Imagine picking up a hymnal and gathering some people to sing parts rather than streaming your favorite tunes next time you find yourself looking for some diversion.

Contemporary revisions of Anglican liturgies have sought to reincorporate biblical songs that have remained in daily prayers in the Roman Catholic Church. In the Anglican Church of Canada, the *Book of Alternative Services*, following the *Book of Common Prayer* for the Episcopal Church, offers several alternative options for the traditional morning and evening prayer canticles mentioned above. There are also new musical settings that attempt to modernize the musical language, and others that attempt to replicate the song of the Israelites. New metrical translations fit to traditional and folk hymns are offered in several recent hymnals. Many congregations also practice responsorial singing, in which a cantor and congregation respond to each other in verse and refrain form. Each of these songs offers us words with which to praise our God with our own particular voices, in our own particular time and place. As we sing these words, given by God for our worship of God, with music from every tongue and tribe throughout history, we are being made into the people of God.

1

Being God's Song:
Venite, Exultemus Domino

Ephraim Radner

O come, let us sing unto the Lord; let us heartily rejoice in the strength of our salvation! With this opening from Psalm 95 we begin our corporate morning prayer at Wycliffe College, joining with countless Christians who have begun their corporate morning prayer since the early church. Perhaps, if we are lucky, we even sing the psalm. That is what I want to touch on in these introductory remarks to *Come, Let Us Sing to the Lord*—that is, singing Scripture.

This volume reflects a preaching series offered by the faculty of Wycliffe College. Some of our preaching series are on a given book of Scripture, like Jeremiah; sometimes they are on some key aspect of the Christian life, like vocation. This series is on the biblical "canticles," that is, on those parts of Scripture we know to be *songs*: the Song of Moses at the Red Sea in Exodus 15, the so-called *Magnificat* or Song of Mary from Luke, and so on. Here I offer a brief reflection on singing the Bible more broadly.

The focus of this reflection is not just singing *in* the Bible, although that's important to get straight too. Obviously singing took place among the peoples of Old and New Testaments. Paul, in Colossians (3:18), urges that "psalms, hymns, and spiritual songs" be sung "with grace in our hearts." People had been doing that for generations. But, as is also obvious, we only have the *words* to a few of these songs that Israelites and early Christians sang. We have no access to the music itself. That we have no divinely inspired music to accompany Scripture is theologically significant, but it has also created problems. We tend to approach the Bible only as a textual document—as words on a page to be read or spoken. In the eighteenth century, people realized that there was such a thing as biblical "poetry."[1] Yet they still treated it as literary critics do, that is, as a form of *speech*. But in pre-literate societies, poetry was probably never spoken as a discourse. It was—and I subscribe to this theory—always sung. If there is poetry in the Bible, we can be sure that it was sung. Not read, but sung.

The Creation of Song

The Bible itself touches on the origin of music. We are told for instance in Gen 4:31 that Jubal, the son of Lamech, was "the father of all those who play the lyre and the pipe." There is, however, no mention of *singing* until Moses stands in triumph over the Egyptians, having passed through the sea, and sings to God (Exod 15:1), a song so famous it is repeated in heaven in the Book of Revelation (Rev 15:3). David, of course, is the paragon of the biblical musician. He is skilled at the lyre and at song-writing, calms the

---

1. For example, see Lowth's *Lectures on the Sacred Poetry of the Hebrews*.

madness of Saul, and composes musical prayers that become the heart of the Psalter, the book of Psalms. David himself, we hear, "invents instruments" for the "praise" of the Lord (1 Chr 23:5), and he personally organizes singers and instrumentalists for the service of the tabernacle and then Temple (1 Chr 6:31; 9:33; 15:16, 19), famously appointing Heman, Asaph, and Ethan as "singers." "Sing to [the Lord] a new song," he writes (or rather, sings). "Play skillfully on the strings, with loud shouts" (Ps 33:3). The beginning of some of the Psalms hint at melodies that were to be used. The word "sing" appears over sixty-five times in the Book of Psalms, not surprisingly.

Singing appears elsewhere too—almost twenty times in the Book of Isaiah, in the most astonishing of ways. To be sure, singing with instruments was also seen, at times, as frivolous and as a sign of sinful dissipation (Isa 5:12; Amos 5:23; 6:5): the lyre, the harp, the timbrel, flutes, song . . . and wine! These passages assume they go together. But this judgment is actually rare in the Bible. Jews and Christians have always, until modern times, seen music as somehow divine in origin. In the sixteenth and seventeenth centuries, an argument developed as to whether music was originally voiced or instrumental. After all, Jubal with his instruments is mentioned before Moses and his tongue. But the consensus landed on the human voice. The philosopher Jean-Jacques Rousseau, some time later, famously speculated that human language itself originated in musical *song*—we sang before we spoke. Common discourse, he argued, is a rationalistic debasement of the heartfelt communication that musical speech primordially had for human beings.

Part of the reason Christian philosophers pressed for voice as more original than instrument was the deep insight that creation itself "sings" to God. Certainly the Psalms and Isaiah tell us this: meadows, trees, hills, birds, even the seas, the very heavens and depths of the earth make song to their Lord (cf. Pss 65:13; 96:12; 98:8; 104:12; 69:34; Isa 44:23, etc). The very act of creation is one upheld by singing. God says to Job: "Where wast thou when I laid the foundations of the earth? declare, if thou hast understanding... When the morning stars sang together, and all the sons of God shouted for joy?" (Job 38:4, 7)

Hence, songs of praise seem to be a part of created being itself. Music precedes not just human speech, but even the *creation* of human beings. That is biblical. Even the ancient Greeks had the idea that the planets themselves make a music according to the proportions of their orbits. This was taken up by Christian thinkers (Boethius), most famously by the seventeenth-century astronomer and mathematician Johannes Kepler.[2] They called it "the music of the spheres"—that harmonious sound of the very universe. While it might seem absurd that planets could make a "sound" in empty space, the ultimate idea was that *God* hears this music, for God has created a world that, in its very being, exists in constant praise of its creator. Isaac Newton's notion of space as a divine "sensorium"—the realm where god perceives creation—catches some of this. In Newton's concept God *feels*—and hears—the sounds of everything he creates. That is in fact what creation *does* in its internal being: it praises God in song. To be alive, to be a creature, is to be a song for God.

---

2. For a much earlier example, see Boethius' *De Musica*.

Singing the Bible

So it must seem odd that in the sixteenth and seventeenth centuries, debates arose among Christians over the place of music in church. Reformed Calvinists were the most contentious. John Calvin himself rejected any use of musical instruments in church as bound too much to the "shadows" of the Old Testament that had now passed away in Christ. And he also seems to have forbidden the singing of non-biblical hymns. Still, he encouraged psalm-singing as a form of liturgical prayer, and had the psalms translated into metrical versions that could be easily followed by the congregation and set to simple tunes. Calvin even commissioned song settings of the Song of Simeon, the Lord's Prayer, the Ten Commandments, and the Apostles' Creed. Imagine singing "Thou shalt not serve a graven image; a jealous God am I, your lord . . . "

But Calvin's Puritan followers in Britain pressed the Old Testament as shadow to the extreme. They were convinced that nothing should be done in church services that was not laid out explicitly in the New Testament. The Old Testament liturgical practices had been abrogated by the New, so that, if Psalms were to be sung, it was not during the liturgy but privately, before or after the service, and only according to a unison tune—no harmony. They were also adamant that prayer itself was to be spontaneous: said from the heart. Thus, to say, let alone sing, something from Scripture as one's *own* prayer was both irreverent and irrelevant. It's not *your* prayer, from *your* heart.

"Nonsense!" replied others. Reformation Christians in England had, since the 1530s, been singing Psalms and biblical canticles in English, with harmony and instruments.³ Richard Hooker became the great respondent to the Puritan critiques. For Hooker, nothing could be more powerful—more transformative—than uttering the very words of Scripture as one's own. Scripture itself was Spirit-filled. And to pray it musically was even better, he said, for it represented the taking of God's own word and creating something beautiful with it, by which God might be adored with his own divine power enabling. To sing the Scriptures was to be joined with the heavenly reality of divine creation itself. On more than one occasion, he noted that when we pray and sing before God together, we do so in "the presence celestial powers, that there we stand, we pray, we sound forth hymns unto God having his Angels intermingled as our associates . . . "⁴ We sing with the "morning stars" and the "sons of God," as Job puts it.

God Sings in Us

Even before the angels themselves open their mouths, God has opened his own in song: "The LORD thy God in the midst of thee [is] mighty; he will save, he will rejoice over thee with joy; he will rest in his love, he will joy over thee with singing" (Zeph 3:17). God sings first. Then Creation sings. Singing Scripture means allowing God's melodic and harmonious truth to touch us in a responsive "chord." The Spirit sees to that. Singing the Scripture is the epitome of what it means to stand before God as his creature. God sings his own word to us in all its formative and creative truth; and we, in turn, are led by God's spirit as it enables

---

3. Coverdale's *Goostly Psalmes and Spirituall Songes* was an influential example of this kind of metrical psalmody.

4. Hooker, *Of the Laws of Ecclesiastical Polity*, V:37–9.

our own particular created being to sing it back in response. That is the world *as it should be.*

"Before the beginning of their prayers," writes St. Athanasius long ago, speaking of the churches he had visited in Constantinople in the early fourth century, "Christians invite and exhort one another in the words of this Psalm [95]": "come let us sing to the Lord a new song, heartily rejoicing." It is preparatory to hearing God's word, in part because, as in its use in Hebrews, it is a call to faithfulness before the Word who is Christ. But its call is a *musical* call, a joining with the most profound aspects of our created being, beginning all prayer—life itself—with praise of God, which is what it means to exist at all.

Venite, Exultemus Domino: Psalm 95 (BCP 1979)

1 O come, let us sing unto the Lord;
   let us heartily rejoice in the strength of our salvation.
2 Let us come before his presence with thanksgiving,
   and show ourselves glad in him with psalms.

3 For the Lord is a great God,
   and a great King above all gods.
4 In his hand are all the corners of the earth,
   and the strength of the hills is his also.
5 The sea is his and he made it,
   and his hands prepared the dry land.

6 O come, let us worship and fall down,
   and kneel before the Lord our Maker.

Come, Let Us Sing to the Lord

   7 For he is the Lord our God;
       and we are the people of his pasture
       and the sheep of his hand.

   8 Today if ye will hear his voice, harden not your hearts
       as in the provocation,
       and as in the day of Temptation in the wilderness;
   9 When your fathers tempted me,
       proved me, and saw my works.
10 Forty years long was I grieved with this generation, and said,
       "It is a people that do err in their hearts,
       for they have not known my ways;
11 Unto whom I sware in my wrath,
       that they should not enter into my rest."

2

Song of Deliverance: *Cantemus Domino*

Peter Robinson

Moses' and Miriam's song is one of praise for deliverance.

I will sing to the Lord for he has triumphed gloriously.

The people of Israel have finally been given permission to leave Egypt. Pharoah, faced with the final plague, the death of the firstborn, relinquishes his grip and allows them to go. They pack quickly and flee, but it isn't long before Pharoah changes his mind and the people of Israel see the powerful Egyptian army pursuing them.

It is a terrifying image—newly minted refugees fleeing for their lives, carrying their small children, weighed down with their belongings, and behind them a dreadful army mounted in chariots approaching at speed. Death is stalking them—there is no escape. But somehow, miraculously, God delivers them. How could they not break out in song and dancing? Praising God that he has delivered them, that he has set them free.

I will sing to the Lord for his glorious triumph;
The horse and rider he has hurled into the sea . . .

> *Your right hand, O Lord, is majestic in power;*
> *Your right hand, O Lord, shatters the enemy.*

They have been saved. But their journey into the wilderness is only just beginning.

The Israelites' Worship

Three days later they arrive at Marah parched and tired; the only water they can find is undrinkable. Exhaustion and despair take over again, fear grips their hearts, and their song of praise turns to grumbling and resentment: "Moses, where is your God?" It is not just the water which is bitter. It is the people themselves: "Your God has abandoned us."

But God once again delivers them. Moses throws a piece of wood on the water and it turns sweet. And as they quench their thirst, you can almost hear the refrain beginning to swell again: "I will sing to the Lord." Indeed, it is not hard to imagine that the people of Israel sing this song again and again in their journey to Mount Sinai, in the wilderness, in their entry into the Promised Land and in the life that follows after.

They are learning to worship God, to respond to him for what he has done and who he is. We catch riffs from this song as it echoes through this story of God at work with his people. Perhaps, particularly in the psalms. *Who is like you, O Lord, among the gods, Holy, awesome, worker of wonders?*

The Song of Moses and Miriam is more than just a song of thanksgiving for God's deliverance from Egypt. It is the appropriate worship of this God who, over and over again, is revealed as faithful and true, as the one God. The song climaxes in verses 16–18: God has formed this people, brought them into his presence, and established that he alone is Lord, Lord over all, forever.

In the Exodus, the people of Israel begin to glimpse the truth of who God is, and in this song they begin to give voice to that truth as their truth, as *the* truth. We can almost hear this song of praise growing richer and deeper as the acts of God's deliverance and provision pile up one upon another.

When We Stop Singing

All of this makes their repeated grumbling, resentment, and rejection of God so unacceptable. When they are overwhelmed by the situations they find themselves in, and fear and despair cause them to cry out in bitterness and anger rather than praise, they are not just being churlish. Refusing to do the right thing and acknowledge God, they are letting go of what is good and beautiful and true. Their inability to continue to sing in praise and worship of God is not just a failure in their duty. It is allowing fear to lead them in a descent into disorder and chaos. The joyful chorus breaks down into shouts of acrimony and anger, noisy gongs and clanging cymbals: it all begins to fall apart.

It is easy to sit in judgment of Israel for their constant doubting and whining. It seems as though they turn away from God mere moments after he has delivered them from yet another enemy or generously provided for their needs. It is easy to judge, except that this is our own experience as well. As great as the delivery out of Egypt was, it is a mere shadow of our delivery from the power of sin and death. Yet, faced with difficulty, with loss, with illness, we too can be quickly overwhelmed with despair. In the midst of chaos, what threatens us can easily appear more powerful than God. All too quickly our praise turns into bitterness. Perhaps what is most sobering is that in North America we often stop singing, or forget to sing God's praise, not because we are threatened, but because we are simply too busy.

This is all further complicated in that God's intention was to show who he was to the whole world through the people of Israel, just as he wants to show himself to the world through us. *When your people, O Lord, passed by, the nations trembled.* When Israel stopped singing, or when we stop singing, the whole world grows more discordant, more dissonant—it turns from melody to noise. Singing God's praise is not simply a duty or an appropriate response to God for what God has done. When the worship of God is at the centre of the coherence of this world—when the trees of the field are able to clap their hands with God's people in praise of the Lord—all things hold together.

How do we keep on singing?

God Sings

Who is like you, O Lord, among the gods,
Holy, awesome, worker of wonders?

In Revelation 15 we hear an echo from this song again, but now it is not just the song of Moses but the song of the Lamb, for he is the one who did not stop singing even in the face of betrayal, loss, and death. Indeed, this has been God's song all along. While Moses may have been the first to sing this song, it was never about him; it was always about God, and now God sings it for us.

The right hand of God, majestic in power, is also the Lamb who shatters the enemy in a way we could not expect: by standing for us when we were unable to stand

and by singing the praise and wonder and truth of God, that God is Lord over all. He overcomes fear and death. He sang this song in a life of obedience, obedience even to the point of death on the cross.

Seated at the right hand of the Father, he now leads us in our song of praise and worship. And we hear the promise first hinted at in Moses' song that all nations, all peoples will finally worship God, because of the Lamb. He sings for us even when we are unable to sing. Because he sings this song it will never be silenced. And because he sings, we too must sing.

So I will sing to the Lord, for he has, and he will, triumph gloriously.

The Song of Moses: Exodus 15:1–3, 6, 11, 13, 17–18 (BAS)

1 I will sing to the Lord for his glorious triumph;
 the horse and the rider he has hurled into the sea.
2 The Lord has become my strength and refuge;
 the Lord himself has become my savior.

He is my God and I will praise him;
 my father's God and I will exalt him.
3 The Lord himself is a mighty warrior;
 the Lord, the Lord is his name.

6 Your right hand, O Lord, is majestic in power;
 your right hand, O Lord, shatters the enemy.
11 Who is like you, O Lord, among the gods,
 holy, awesome, worker of wonders?

Come, Let Us Sing to the Lord

13 In steadfast love you led your people,
   you guided your redeemed with your great strength.
17 You brought them in safety to your holy place,
   and planted them firm on your own mountain.
   You brought them into your own house.
18 The Lord shall reign for ever and ever.

3

Of God's Victory: The Song of Deborah

Marion Taylor

THE SONG OF DEBORAH in Judges chapter 5 celebrates in poetry the story narrated first in prose in Judges 4. The victory Deborah celebrates marks the end of twenty years of cruel oppression under King Jabin of Canaan—oppression that was viewed as punishment for doing what "was evil in the sight of the Lord, after the judge Ehud died" (Judg 4:1). Deborah praises the leaders who stepped up to the plate and got involved and the people who followed them. She criticizes the tribes who were indecisive, who hung back or refused to get involved at all. Like many others, Barak was very reluctant to get involved in battling the Canaanite king, Jabin of Hazor. Deborah, a prophetess, had sent Barak the message that the Lord, the God of Israel, commanded him to "go, and take with him ten thousand men of Naphtali and Zebulun and lead them up to Mount Tabor," to fight against Sisera, who led Jabin's very well equipped forces (Ju 4:6–7). Barak agreed to go only if Deborah went with him. For his conditional obedience, Barak was denied the glory of the victory and shamed. As Deborah prophesied, the Lord would sell Sisera into the hand of a woman. That woman of course was Jael, whom Deborah praises as "most blessed of women" (Ju 5: 7, 24).

This rather bloody story is part of the larger story of Israel's taking of the land, settling of the land, defiling of the land, and eventual exile and return to the land. Stories of the taking and possessing of the land are particularly unpalatable to many modern readers of Scripture. When I read Judges 5 with a group of women at church, many responded that they had not read this story in a long time, and that they did not like this story, particularly the gory parts.

Modern readers are not the only ones who have been troubled by this story. Readers through history wrestled with the question of what to make of Deborah—a female judge, prophet, singer, and warrior who called herself "a mother in Israel." They were even more puzzled by Jael's bloody assassination of Sisera. And Sisera's mother was also troubling as she is depicted as anxiously awaiting her son's return—only to be reminded by her maids that he along with his warriors would be dividing the spoil, a womb or two for every man (Ju 5:28–30).

Nineteenth-Century Interpreters of Deborah's Story

The history of the interpretation of Judges 5 shows us that most readers have traditionally ignored, eliminated, or re-interpreted the story "so as to fit their own conceptions of what women could and did achieve in history."[1] Almost every aspect of Deborah's identity elicited comments by

1. Schroeder, *Deborah's Daughters*, 3, citing Israeli historian Tal Ilan.

nineteenth-century readers. Her identity as civil leader and judge, for example, was used by some to justify claims that women could hold positions of political and religious power and authority. According to one male Methodist minister and women rights' advocate writing in 1887, "the position of [Deborah] appears to have been much the same as that of president of the United States, with the additional functions of the judicial and religious offices of the nation. Hence this woman [Deborah] was President, Supreme Judge, and Right Reverend in the Theocratic Republic of Israel."[2]

Others who opposed women's public leadership explained that Deborah's role was exceptional. Nineteenth-century commentator Elizabeth Baxter was very troubled by Deborah's public leadership and viewed her as an exception, arguing that she had to lead because the men were not carrying out their God-given leadership roles.[3] Grace Aguilar (1816–47), Clara Balfour (1808–78), and Julia McNair Wright (1840–1903) praised Deborah's intelligence as a judge and poet, assumed she was well educated, and used her example as an argument for equal education for women.[4]

But Deborah was not the only woman to elicit great comment in the nineteenth century. Jael's inhospitable, duplicitous, and unladylike actions ran counter to shared expectations that women are "peacemakers, nurturers, trustworthy, hospitable and passive in the realm of politics

2. Ibid., 4.

3. See Baxter, *The Women in the Word*, 72–82, as cited in Taylor and de Groot, *Women of War*, 105–10.

4. Taylor and de Groot, *Women of War*, 77. Grace Aguilar was a prolific Jewish writer, Clara Balfour an English lecturer and writer, and Julia McNair Wright an American educator.

and war."[5] Renowned social activist Elizabeth Cady Stanton (1815–1902) regarded Jael's action as "more like the work of a fiend than of a woman."[6] But what of Deborah's very high praise of Jael, as most blessed of women? Most interpreters who had high regard for the authority of Scripture felt a need to justify Jael's conduct. To explain why Jael's actions were valorized, many interpreters pointed to differences between primitive and enlightened cultures and between times of peace and times of war. According to English Jewish educators, Annie de Rothschild (1844–1926) and Constance de Rothschild (1843–1931), treason "was accepted and even praised by an oppressed and struggling people in that early dawn of civilization."[7] Others drew on situational ethics. One early Anglican revisionist, Anne Mercier (1843–1917) boldly stated that Deborah was wrong in her valuation of Jael as most blessed of women, and she explained it away as being part of Deborah's post-battle enthusiasm that led her to sing an uninspired song.[8]

But Deborah's song does more than shame men who refused to fight God's battles and praise male and female warriors fighting against God's enemies. It also acknowledges the female victims of war. Harriet Beecher Stowe (1811–96) is one of a number of early interpreters who developed the theme of violence against women as a way to justify Jael's bloody actions. Stowe argued that Jael killed

5. Ibid., 114–15.

6. Stanton, "The Book of Judges, Chapter II," 20–21, as cited in Taylor and de Groot, *Women of War*, 153.

7. De Rothschild and de Rothschild, *The History and Literature of the Israelites*, 286. As cited in Taylor and de Groot, *Women of War*, 138.

8. Mercier, *The Story of Salvation*, 112; cf. 149, "Deborah was Wrong about Jael."

the tiger, Sisera, who ravished women and children, and in doing so she prevented the deaths of those Sisera and his men would have raped.[9]

Deborah's song in Judges 5 inspired many to reflect on important issues related to women's roles, women's education, and even the timely question of violence against women in times of war. It also provoked many to find the story's religious and moral significance in allegorical or typological readings of aspects of the story. British Anglican educator Etty Woosnam (1849–ca. 1883) calls all her readers to "be a spiritual Jael and nail down to the ground her Sisera [that is] . . . coldness and hardness of heart and our grievous besetting sins."[10] The pseudonymous Anglo-Catholic writer M. G. similarly calls readers to fight Sisera and the Canaanites—who are figures for Satan and his army—and to fight then "as bravely as men."[11] A more negative figural reading of Jael picks up on her duplicity and sees her as "a type of worldly pleasure, which promises only to betray; it also presents Sisera . . . [as] a type of those who trust for happiness in the things of this world."[12]

Deborah Points to God

I find all these readings interesting and provocative. Sometimes they tell us more about the interpreters than the text. They remind us of how creative our foremothers and

9. Stowe, *Woman in Sacred History*, 83–90, as cited in Taylor and de Groot, *Women of War*, 138–40.

10. Woosnam, *The Women of the Bible*, 97–109, as cited in Taylor and de Groot, *Women of War*, 145.

11. M. G., *Women Like Ourselves*, 60–66, as cited in Taylor and de Groot, *Women of War*, 151.

12. Smith, *The Battles of the Bible*, 111–15, as cited in Taylor and de Groot, *Women of War*, 131.

fathers were sometimes as they tried to make moral and spiritual sense of out a song that celebrates victory over the Canaanites, that valorizes those who fought, and shames those who refused to fight—a song that praises women in leadership and heroic duplicity, and calls attention to the practice of raping women after battle.

These readings also force us back to the ancient Song of Deborah itself, where a close reading reveals that the primary focus on Deborah's song is celebration of God's victory. To be sure, human actors in the story of God's victory are celebrated, but none of the deliverers could have taken decisive actions without the actions of all the other players—Barak, Deborah, Jael, and the men who courageously battled Jabin's forces were all needed to bring victory. But ultimately, as Deborah's song celebrates, the victory given to Israel was God's. In verse 4 the Lord is the one leading the army:

> LORD, when *you* went out from Seir,
>
> when *you* marched from the region of Edom,
>
> the earth trembled
>
> and the heavens dropped,
>
> yes, the clouds dropped water.

It was God's battle and they were God's warriors. The defeat of the enemies—including Sisera, who died at Jael's hand—was God's victory. The poem concludes:

> "So may all your enemies perish, O LORD!
>
> But your friends be like the sun as he rises in his might."
>
> And the land had rest for forty years.

In Deborah's Song, then, we celebrate God's victory. God gives his faithful people a victory that led to forty years of peace in the land God had promised long before to his people. Deborah's victory song, which scholars agree is older than the prose account and likely among the oldest passages in the Old Testament, continues to speak to us today.

God's Call

One of the women in my Bible study who was finding the pressures of life and ministry overwhelming felt encouraged by this text: "Awake, Awake Deborah, Awake, awake and sing a song, Arise Barak." Our call is not to a battle against the Canaanites to repossess the land taken away because of disobedience. The conquest of Canaan happened once and it is no more. But God's people's battles are not over. They are battles for truth, righteousness, and justice. Many Christians today face threatening battles at every turn, both inside and outside the church. The Song of Deborah calls us to remember that when God calls us to awake and arise to battle real and spiritual enemies, we are not alone. These are the Lord's battles.

Judges 5 is not the end of the story of God. We look forward to the book of Revelation and John's vision of the ultimate battle, which Jesus as bridegroom fought and won. There too the ultimate victory for the Lamb is celebrated in song. Eugene Peterson's paraphrase of Revelation 19 in his translation *The Message* is particularly evocative:

> 1 I heard a sound like massed choirs in Heaven singing, Hallelujah! The salvation and glory and power are God's—

> 2 his judgments true, his judgments just. He judged the great Whore who corrupted the earth with her lust. He avenged on her the blood of his servants.
>
> 3 Then, more singing: Hallelujah! The smoke from her burning billows up to high Heaven forever and ever and ever.
>
> 4 The Twenty-four Elders and the Four Animals fell to their knees and worshiped God on his Throne, praising, Amen! Yes! Hallelujah!
>
> 5 From the Throne came a shout, a command: Praise our God, all you his servants, All you who fear him, small and great!
>
> 6 Then I heard the sound of massed choirs, the sound of a mighty cataract, the sound of strong thunder: Hallelujah! The Master reigns, our God, the Sovereign-Strong!
>
> 7 Let us celebrate, let us rejoice, let us give him the glory! The Marriage of the Lamb has come. (Rev 19:1–7 MSG)

I conclude with Spurgeon's comments on Judges 5, which call us to go forth giving thanks to Jesus our Lord Christ for our deliverance from sin and death. Thus Spurgeon writes, "Deborah sang concerning the overthrow of Israel's enemies, and the deliverance vouchsafed to the tribes: we have a far richer theme for music; we have been delivered from worse enemies, and saved by a greater salvation. Let our gratitude be deeper; let our song be more jubilant."[13]

---

13. Charles Spurgeon preached a sermon on Deborah's Song on July 28, 1867; see http://www.spurgeon.org/sermons/0763.php.

The Song of Deborah: Judges 5:2–31
(New Revised Standard Version)

2 When locks are long in Israel,
   when the people offer themselves willingly—
   bless the Lord!

3 Hear, O kings; give ear, O princes;
   to the Lord I will sing,
   I will make melody to the Lord, the God of Israel.

4 Lord, when you went out from Seir,
   when you marched from the region of Edom,
the earth trembled,
   and the heavens poured,
   the clouds indeed poured water.
5 The mountains quaked before the Lord, the One of Sinai,
   before the Lord, the God of Israel.

6 In the days of Shamgar son of Anath,
   in the days of Jael, caravans ceased
   and travellers kept to the byways.
7 The peasantry prospered in Israel,
   they grew fat on plunder,
because you arose, Deborah,
   arose as a mother in Israel.
8 When new gods were chosen,
   then war was in the gates.
Was shield or spear to be seen
   among forty thousand in Israel?

Come, Let Us Sing to the Lord

> 9 My heart goes out to the commanders of Israel
> who offered themselves willingly among the people.
> Bless the Lord.

> 10 Tell of it, you who ride on white donkeys,
> you who sit on rich carpets,
> and you who walk by the way.
> 11 To the sound of musicians at the watering-places,
> there they repeat the triumphs of the Lord,
> the triumphs of his peasantry in Israel.

Then down to the gates marched the people of the Lord.

> 12 Awake, awake, Deborah!
> Awake, awake, utter a song!
> Arise, Barak, lead away your captives,
> O son of Abinoam.
> 13 Then down marched the remnant of the noble;
> the people of the Lord marched down for him against the mighty.
> 14 From Ephraim they set out into the valley,
> following you, Benjamin, with your kin;
> from Machir marched down the commanders,
> and from Zebulun those who bear the marshal's staff;
> 15 the chiefs of Issachar came with Deborah,
> and Issachar faithful to Barak;
> into the valley they rushed out at his heels.
> Among the clans of Reuben
> there were great searchings of heart.
> 16 Why did you tarry among the sheepfolds,
> to hear the piping for the flocks?

Among the clans of Reuben
    there were great searchings of heart.
17 Gilead stayed beyond the Jordan;
    and Dan, why did he abide with the ships?
Asher sat still at the coast of the sea,
    settling down by his landings.
18 Zebulun is a people that scorned death;
    Naphtali too, on the heights of the field.

19 The kings came, they fought;
    then fought the kings of Canaan,
at Taanach, by the waters of Megiddo;
    they got no spoils of silver.
20 The stars fought from heaven,
    from their courses they fought against Sisera.
21 The torrent Kishon swept them away,
    the onrushing torrent, the torrent Kishon.
    March on, my soul, with might!

22 Then loud beat the horses' hoofs
    with the galloping, galloping of his steeds.

23 Curse Meroz, says the angel of the Lord,
    curse bitterly its inhabitants,
because they did not come to the help of the Lord,
    to the help of the Lord against the mighty.

24 Most blessed of women be Jael,
    the wife of Heber the Kenite,
    of tent-dwelling women most blessed.
25 He asked water and she gave him milk,
    she brought him curds in a lordly bowl.

26 She put her hand to the tent-peg
   and her right hand to the workmen's mallet;
she struck Sisera a blow,
   she crushed his head,
   she shattered and pierced his temple.
27 He sank, he fell,
   he lay still at her feet;
at her feet he sank, he fell;
   where he sank, there he fell dead.

28 Out of the window she peered,
   the mother of Sisera gazed through the lattice:
"Why is his chariot so long in coming?
   Why tarry the hoofbeats of his chariots?"
29 Her wisest ladies make answer,
   indeed, she answers the question herself:
30 "Are they not finding and dividing the spoil?—
   A girl or two for every man;
spoil of dyed stuffs for Sisera,
   spoil of dyed stuffs embroidered,
   two pieces of dyed work embroidered for my neck as spoil?"

31 So perish all your enemies, O Lord!
   But may your friends be like the sun as it rises in its might.

4

All Creation Sings: *Benedicite Omnia Opera*

Thomas P. Power

Not all Songs of Scripture are canticles, but many, including the subject of this meditation, are. The term "canticle" derives from the Latin *canticum*, meaning song. Canticles as songs derived from the Bible have different themes and uses. They have been used traditionally as a call to worship and as responses to readings since the early centuries of the church.

The most widely used canticles in Christian worship over the centuries are four in number: the *Benedictus* or Zechariah's song (Luke 1:68–79), Mary's *Magnificat* (Luke 1:46–55), the *Nunc dimittis* or Song of Simeon (Luke 2:29–32), all three found in the gospel of Luke. The fourth one, examined here, is the *Benedicite* or Song of the Three Young Men, so called from its opening words in Latin, *Benedicite omnia opera* or "Bless all the works."

The Church's Use

The text of the *Benedicite* is not part of the canon of Scripture. The passage is omitted from Protestant Bibles because it is viewed as part of the apocryphal tradition. And so, because it belongs in the apocrypha, it is regarded as optional or as an addition.

Yet despite its origin as a non-canonical source, it has been included in the *Book of Common Prayer*. At the time of the Reformation, the Church of England retained the three canticles from Luke. It also retained the *Benedicite* as an alternative to the *Te Deum* in the order of service for morning prayer, where it can be used following the first scripture lesson.

Although non-canonical, this canticle along with the apocrypha in general is seen to have some value for believers. As article 6 of the Thirty-nine Articles of Religion says of such apocryphal works: "The Church doth read [them] for example of life and instruction of manners; but yet doth not apply them to establish any doctrine."[1] The Church uses this canticle in its liturgy because of its belief that, though deriving from the apocryphal tradition, it can be useful for "example of life and instruction of manners."

From the Fiery Furnace

In the apocryphal version, the text is inserted between verses 23 and 24 of Daniel 3. Verse 23 says: "And these three men [that is, Shadrach, Meshach, and Abednego] firmly tied, fell into the blazing fire." Then follows the insert of the *Benedicite*, the words of which are put into the mouths of Daniel's three friends. You will recall that they

---

1. BCP, "Articles of Religion," Article 6, p. 700.

had been cast into the furnace by king Nebuchadnezzar as punishment for their refusal to worship the golden image he had devised of himself. Their song is a hymn of praise as they stand unconsumed in the furnace.

Song of the Created Order

The canticle is an invitation to praise and is a song of creation. It is a call for all that God has created to praise him. Each verse names a feature of the created order of the world.

Given the parameters for its usefulness to the church discussed earlier, what is there in this canticle that is worthy for "example of life and instruction of manners"?

Three observations may be made. Firstly, here together we have a solicitation of the works of the Lord, in heaven and on earth, to bless the Creator. So the waters, the sun, moon and stars, winter and summer, showers, winds, fire, heat, nights and days, light and darkness, and all living things—in all their variety, form, and splendor—are invoked into a chorus of thanks and praise to God the Creator. The canticle progresses through the natural phenomena to humanity in general, through God's chosen few, up to the Three whose deliverance is supposed to have called forth this hymn of praise. The hymn is given unity by a refrain ("Bless ye the Lord, praise him and magnify him forever") repeated after each line, emphasizing that the Lord is the consistent object of blessing and praise. The canticle has a psalm-like quality, and in this echoes for instance Psalms 136 and 148, which have a similar litany format and theme.

Secondly, the canticle is a reminder that God reveals himself by two different books: in Scripture and the book of creation. The canticle celebrates the book of creation as a manifestation of God's glory and power. Calvin expresses well God's purpose in authoring the book of creation:

> In every part of the world, he has written and as it were engraven the glory of his power, goodness, and eternity . . . For all creatures, from the firmament even to the centre of the earth, could be witnesses and messengers of his glory to all [men], drawing them on to seek him and, having found him, to do him service and honor according to the dignity of a Lord so good, so potent, so wise and everlasting . . . For the little singing birds sang of God, the animals acclaimed Him, the elements feared and the mountains resounded with Him, the river and springs threw glances toward Him, the grasses and flowers smiled.[2]

This canticle is a reminder of divine revelation in creation.

Thirdly, not only do we have an itemization of the elements in creation, physical and human, but also collectively these invocations represent a challenge to the claims of Nebuchadnezzar to be worshipped and his authority acknowledged. In its catalogue of all the created order, driven home by the repetition of "Bless ye the Lord, praise him and magnify him forever" after each, the canticle is a counter to the king's power and might, to the claim that only under him is there security and order and prosperity. The canticle affirms God's created order as preeminent over the claims of worldly power.

---

2. Calvin, *Institutes* 1:14, quoted in Santmire, *The Travail of Nature*, 128.

POWER—*ALL CREATION SINGS*: BENEDICITE OMNIA OPERA

God's Victory against Oppression

For Daniel and the Jews in exile under the oppressive power of this king, God appeared absent in their plight. Until, that is, God appeared in time to rescue the three youths.

This canticle can be a hymn of praise for us too when there are demands on our allegiance, when we are forced to bow down before the idolatrous gods of our age in all their oppressiveness. The canticle exemplifies how we can experience the victory of God in trying circumstances or as an expression of faith in God, in times when he appears absent. In these ways the canticle is an appropriate one for "example of life and instruction in manners."

The Song of the Three Children: Daniel 3:57-87 (BCP1979)

57 O all ye works of the Lord, bless ye the Lord;
praise him and magnify him for ever.
58 O ye angels of the Lord, bless ye the Lord;
praise him and magnify him for ever.

59 O ye heavens, bless ye the Lord;
60 O ye waters that be above the firmament, bless ye the Lord;
61 O all ye powers of the Lord, bless ye the Lord;
praise him and magnify him for ever.

62 O ye sun and moon, bless ye the Lord;
63 O ye stars of heaven, bless ye the Lord;
64 O ye showers and dew, bless ye the Lord;
praise him and magnify him for ever.

Come, Let Us Sing to the Lord

65 O ye winds of God, bless ye the Lord;
66 O ye fire and heat, bless ye the Lord;
67 O ye winter and summer, bless ye the Lord;
    praise him and magnify him for ever.

68 O ye dews and frosts, bless ye the Lord;
69 O ye frost and cold, bless ye the Lord;
70 O ye ice and snow, bless ye the Lord;
    praise him and magnify him for ever.

71 O ye nights and days, bless ye the Lord;
72 O ye light and darkness, bless ye the Lord;
73 O ye lightnings and clouds, bless ye the Lord;
    praise him and magnify him for ever.

74 O let the earth bless the Lord;
75 O ye mountains and hills, bless ye the Lord;
76 O all ye green things upon the earth, bless ye the Lord;
    praise him and magnify him for ever.

77 O ye wells, bless ye the Lord;
78 O ye seas and floods, bless ye the Lord;
79 O ye whales and all that move in the waters, bless ye the Lord;
    praise him and magnify him for ever.

80 O all ye fowls of the air, bless ye the Lord;
81 O all ye beasts and cattle, bless ye the Lord;
82 O ye children of men, bless ye the Lord;
    praise him and magnify him for ever.

Power—*All Creation Sings:* Benedicite Omnia Opera

83 O ye people of God, bless the Lord;
84 O ye priests of the Lord, bless ye the Lord;
85 O ye servants of the Lord, bless ye the Lord;
   praise him and magnify him for ever.

86 O ye spirits and souls of the righteous, bless ye the Lord;
87 O ye holy and humble men of heart, bless ye the Lord.
Let us bless the Father, the Son, and the Holy Spirit;
   praise him and magnify him for ever.

5

A Lament: How the Mighty Have Fallen

Annette Brownlee

The death of Saul, the first king of Israel, spans the division between the first and second books of Samuel. The end of 1 Samuel describes how Israel's enemy, the Amalekites, deal with Saul. They defeat him in battle, which leads to Saul falling on his own sword, ending his own life. The beginning of 2 Samuel describes how David responds to Saul's sad death. He sings a lament.

The shepherd boy who sang while tending Jesse's sheep now sings in sorrow for the death of Saul and his friend, Jonathan. We are told his lament is not a song for himself. "David intoned this lamentation over Saul and his son Jonathan. He ordered that the Song of the Bow be taught to the people of Judah; it is written in the Book of Jashar." The unknown book of poetry, sometimes called the Book of the Upright, is mentioned in only one other place in the Bible: the Book of Joshua, where we are told it describes Joshua's military exploits in Canaan.

David instructed that this lamentation, the Song of the Bow, be persevered for future generations. And taught to the people of Judah. Perhaps we could name it a lament in the school of the Lord. In it the circle of David's lament widens beyond the people of Judah. His enemies are taught what to do, so too their land.

It is a haunting and beautiful song of sorrow for Saul and Jonathan:

They who in life were swifter than eagles, stronger than the lions now lie fallen. The shield of Saul anointed with oil no more, the sword of Saul returned empty, the bow of Jonathan not turned back.

Your glory, oh Israel, lies slain upon your high places. How the Mighty have fallen.

Let there be no dew or rain upon the mountains of Gilboa.

Tell it not in Gath, proclaim it not in the streets of Ashkelon lest the daughters of the Philistines rejoice.

But daughters of Israel weep over Saul.

How the mighty have fallen in the midst of the battle.

The Truth about Saul

Those who know even the briefest outline of Saul's disastrous kingship and lethal jealousy toward his protégé, David, know that this lament is no model for our own funeral eulogies. This Saul seems unrecognizable as the man described in the thirty-one chapters of 1 Samuel. Are we even at the right funeral?

I take my clue for how to make sense of this incongruity from two details in the portion of chapter 1 of 2 Samuel which precedes the lament. First, there is David's insistence that this lament be preserved for generations and taught to the people. This is no personal song of "Ding, dong, the witch is dead." David's eyes are fixed on a wider horizon.

The second detail hints at why David's lament leaves out so much of Saul's life. David is in Ziklag when he receives the news of Saul's death. What was he doing in Ziklag? He had fled there, to this dusty, one-stoplight town on the border between Judah and the lands of the Philistines, to escape Saul's pursuit of him. He hopes Saul won't look for him there. "Saul will despair of seeking me any longer within the borders of Israel, and I shall escape out of his hand."

What is David's response to Saul's jealousy of him—his lethal jealousy? David, who slew Goliath? Who slew tens of thousands of Philistines to Saul's thousands? It is a refusal to do any violence to Saul. He will protect himself only by dodging and running from Saul—even to Ziklag. He won't protect himself by violence—even when he has the chance, he refuses. When Saul walks unarmed into the cave where David and his men are hiding, not only does David not kill him. He bows to the ground and prays, "May the Lord avenge me but I shall not take your life" (1 Sam 24:8).

As in his life, so in his lament, David will do no violence to Saul. Either with the sword or song. For Saul is the Lord's anointed. He is God's choice—his instrument of his purposes.

Our Fallenness, God's Purposes

David understands how God's purposes are carried out: through God's chosen and flawed vessels. Like the morning light which inches along the cracked and warped floorboards of our homes, so too God's purposes work through human history. God uses even our sin and disobedience. My ways are not your ways, says the Lord (Isa 55:8). And so David will not force his ways on the Lord's anointed. If he is to become king—and he will—it will only be through God's ways, not his own.

Rather, David sings, and preserves for us to sing, this reality that is as certain as God's purposes.

The mighty will fall. Even the glory of Israel. All of them. All of us. How do the mighty fall? The story of Saul counts the ways: jealously, impatience with God, an unwillingness to listen to God, disobedience, and on and on. David is a better king than Saul. David listens to God, unlike Saul, but he too will stumble, as do so many kings who come after him. But we are not to rejoice in their downfall or rejoice in the wrong. Rejoicing at others' wrong—at the fallenness—is not God's ways. For we too will fall, or at least stumble, but God will use it.

This is worth preserving for generations, this knowledge and refusal in the face of it to deride those who have fallen. We should sing it—especially given our base public and ecclesial discourse. It was, in fact, sung for generations: a Latin motet from the sixteenth century, an anthem by George Frideric Handel for the funeral of Queen Caroline. Henry Dunster, the first president of Harvard and later a Puritan heretic because he was in favor of infant baptism, probably collected a set of psalms and biblical canticles, including "How are the mighty fallen." It became the most popular psalm and hymn book in early New England. The anthem "The beauty of Israel is slain / How are the mighty fallen," became a favorite text in New England in the early eighteenth century.

We need not do violence to those who have fallen, even our enemies, with weapon or words, trumpet or tongue. David has taught us where this all leads. We know where this all leads. It leads to the one who comes from his house, from David's own lineage with its cracked and warped line of kings. It leads to Jesus Christ. Jesus will stumble, literally stumble as he carries his cross. Jesus, Israel's glory, too will be slain in the high places. Jesus too will fall. And oh, we know how God uses his fallenness.

David's Lament: 2 Samuel 1:19–27 (New Revised Standard Version)

19 Your glory, O Israel, lies slain upon your high places!
 How the mighty have fallen!
20 Tell it not in Gath,
 proclaim it not in the streets of Ashkelon;
or the daughters of the Philistines will rejoice,
 the daughters of the uncircumcised will exult.

21 You mountains of Gilboa,
 let there be no dew or rain upon you,
 nor bounteous fields!
For there the shield of the mighty was defiled,
 the shield of Saul, anointed with oil no more.

22 From the blood of the slain,
 from the fat of the mighty,
the bow of Jonathan did not turn back,
 nor the sword of Saul return empty.

23 Saul and Jonathan, beloved and lovely!
 In life and in death they were not divided;
they were swifter than eagles,
 they were stronger than lions.

Brownlee—*A Lament: How the Mighty Have Fallen*

24 O daughters of Israel, weep over Saul,
    who clothed you with crimson, in luxury,
    who put ornaments of gold on your apparel.

25 How the mighty have fallen
    in the midst of the battle!

Jonathan lies slain upon your high places.
    26 I am distressed for you, my brother Jonathan;
greatly beloved were you to me;
    your love to me was wonderful,
    passing the love of women.
27 How the mighty have fallen,
    and the weapons of war perished!

6

Fearless Heralds: The Song of Good News

J. Glen Taylor

As these three verses remind us so eloquently, we Christians are supposed to be heralds of Good News. We are to proclaim not just that God is alive and well, but that He is coming to set things right with the world. As with the prophet of old, we Christians are to shout from the mountaintops: "God is coming. He is graciously making a beeline for us."

Yet there lies within us a nagging sort of feeling that it can't be that simple. (Or can it be?) As the old saying goes, "if it sounds too good to be true, it probably is." So, today when we hear (much less proclaim!) "Good News," people are often suspicious. Rather than listen we are more likely to ask "what's the catch?" or "what's in it for you that you aren't telling me about?" I fear that such skepticism has taken its toll on us bearers of glad tidings, either because we anticipate the suspicion of others or perhaps even because we share it.

There are other reasons why we bearers of glad tidings are reluctant to speak up and out. For one thing, proclaiming even good news has become controversial in our postmodern culture. Why? Because it implies that what is good news for some is likely to be good news for others. (There is the also the issue whether what is called "news" has any meaning or significance apart from those who want to draw our attention to it, which is likely for the purpose of exerting power over us.) And for another thing, many people today find the notion of a God of Good News hard to reconcile with the existence of unbridled evil and violence in the world.

So, who is up for the job of herald of Good News who shouts from mountaintops? The prophet was. And so too, I believe, should we.

The Prophet Speaks the Truth

Suspicion and dubiety are not new. The thirty-nine chapters that come before our song of Good News make it abundantly clear that the people who lived in Isaiah's time were as averse to being gullible as we are today. The odds that Good News was true or easy to believe seemed about as good then as now. Not even Isaiah himself was likely to bet on God's news being good, because earlier in this prophetic book God commissioned Isaiah to proclaim a message of irreversible Bad News to an earlier generation of inhabitants of these same places: Zion, Jerusalem, and the cities of Judah.

Neither does the prophet dodge the nasty problem that God allowed horrible things to happen, which they did to the same earlier generation of Judahites. Isaiah unabashedly attributes the devastation that Assyria and then Babylon brought upon the people of Judah to God's punishment for the Judaeans' sins. Though unpopular today,

Isaiah's explanation of sin is a plausible reason for the calamity that befell Judah in this particular case.

We see in Isaiah then not a naïve idealist who always proclaims Good News but a sober realist who at one time proclaimed Bad News and who now at another time proclaims Good News. No one can accuse Isaiah of not seeing enough hard times to be able to recognize a Good Thing when he sees it. More than seeing hard times, he predicted them, and now does the same with his call for a herald of Good News.

Given how new the relativism of postmodernity might appear to be, it might surprise us to notice that Isaiah does his share of relativizing too. Thus, just prior to the Song of Good News, Isaiah speaks of the transitory nature of humanity and empires relative to the one true God and his word. And yet none of this insight lowers the volume on Isaiah's call for heralds to proclaim the Good News of God.

I want to suggest that we Christians be the very thing Isaiah is calling for: someone unabashedly to share the Good News. So good is this news that it is worth shouting from the mountaintops, as it were. Where will people today hear this true and joyous word of the living God if Christians relinquish their privilege and calling to be heralds of Good News?

The Prophet is Fearless

But what about the pitfalls? In true prophetic form, Isaiah does not pander much to our reservations. (He does acknowledge our fear, but only to say as much as "get over it!") He focuses instead on the sure and changeless nature of God's own testimony, his Word. And surely Isaiah's focus is right, given how transitory we (and our vain aspirations) are in comparison to the life-giving self-revelation of God.

And yet we often remain reluctant to proclaim the Good News. What then is holding us back? Isaiah has identified one thing: fear. But there isn't much reason for Christians in North America to fear.

Let me illustrate. Not long ago a Christian student from overseas noticed a widespread reluctance among Canadian Christians to openly share their faith in Christ within Canada. I believe he was right to attribute this reluctance to fear. Such fear made no sense to this foreign student, for in his country, unlike in Canada, people had reason to be afraid of sharing the Good News: persecution and sometimes death. This student is right to wonder what could possibly justify the fear we often seem to show.

Another reason for our seeming hesitancy is perhaps a doubt in the truth of God's word. But even if we were to question or doubt God's word in some cases, why do so here where these words resonate so clearly with those of John the Baptist who appeared in the wilderness and called upon people to make room for the coming of God's kingly rule, a rule which Jesus, the eternal Son of God, inaugurated in Himself along with words and miraculous deeds?

I hope that by now our reasons not to be heralds of glad tidings are dissipating, yet some might remain with reference to relativism of one sort or another. But here again Isaiah has insight that rings true where he reminds us that the very things that can still lure us away from God—namely personal vanity and empire building akin to that of Assyria or Babylon—are here one day and gone the next. (In the preceding verses Isaiah compares people and empires to grass that withers and flowers that fade.) Indeed, as I write this meditation my ninety-seven-year-old mother, the same woman who seventy years before turned the heads of almost every man who noticed her, becomes with each passing week a more pale and frail shell of her former self. "The grass withers, the flower fades, yet the Word of our God abides forever."

In contrast to all other things that are transitory, Isaiah draws our attention to that which alone is sure, true, and everlasting: the unchanging God whose word abides forever.

God and his word being what they are, what could be more true and everlasting?

Brothers and sisters in Christ, with the coming of Jesus Christ, we have Good News to share with the world. By God's grace and in the power of the Holy Spirit, let us proclaim this real, true, and eternal Good News with joy.

After all, who doesn't like sharing (or hearing) Good News?

The Song of Good News: Isaiah 40:9–11 (Author's translation)

Take yourself up to a high peak,

Herald of Good News for Zion.

Raise your voice high and strong,

Herald of Good News for Jerusalem.

Raise it up with no fear,

Proclaim to the cities of Judah: "Look, it's your God!"

Behold, the Lord Yahweh shall come with might,

Ruling with his own right arm.

And, behold, with him is payment,

Before him is work's reward.

7

The Dawn of Salvation: *Benedictus*

Stephen G. W. Andrews

> And thou, child, shalt be called the Prophet of the Highest: for thou shalt go before the face of the Lord to prepare his ways; to give knowledge of salvation unto his people for the remission of their sins (Luke 1:76–77).

Even the secular historians say that he was a sensation. I don't mean Jesus. In fact, Jesus was one of many pilgrims who ventured into the Jordan River valley to see "the Prophet of the Highest." Talk about spectacles. This guy had the wild-eyed look of a psychic. Dressed in a camel's hair tunic and dining on grasshoppers and wild honey, he tilted at the Jewish government and called people to bewail their wicked ways. He rated high in the entertainment section as a local novelty, and crowds flocked to the Jordan River to witness the bizarre drama of this guy submerging his converts in the swiftly flowing water.

Some undoubtedly found the display to be an interesting diversion. But there were also those who were alarmed by the strange events in the wilderness. Members of the religious establishment in particular were unsettled by the Baptizer's activities. They seemed to get upset when called "a brood of vipers" (Luke 3:7), and they were offended by the apparent slight to their family pedigree—"raising up stones from Abraham," indeed (3:7)! But more ominous to them was the possibility that this charismatic figure could fan the embers of Jewish revolt and arouse the military attention of their Roman overlords.

One can see how John the Baptist became a polarising figure; how, in fact, his very appearance and behavior could be a source of hope for some, while being a threat to others. Scripture elsewhere gives us more angles on who he was. St. Mark claims that he was the long-awaited prophet Elijah (Mark 9:13). Who would have guessed this just by watching his actions and hearing his ravings? And yet it was all just preliminary to the controversy that came to be associated with one of the individuals who would appear before him in order to undergo his baptism.

And so it is that the figure of John the Baptist occupies a central place in the Gospel story. He is the bridge that connects the narrative of God's work in the Old Testament with the new thing God was about to do in the world through his Son. In fact, from the earliest decades of the Church's daily worship, the canticle called the Song of Zechariah, or the *Benedictus* as it is better known, was the canticle that followed the morning's second Bible reading.[1] It expresses the conviction that, as St. Augustine said, *Novum Testamentum in Vetere latet, Vetus Testamentum in Novo patet* ("the New Testament is in the Old concealed; the Old Testament is in the New revealed").[2]

---

1. One of the opening canticles at Lauds, the *Benedictus*, has been part of the Church's liturgy since at least the sixth century.

2. *Quaest. in Heptateuch*, ii.73.

God Re-members

Zechariah's Song proclaims a vision of a God who has never forgotten his people: "To perform the mercy *promised* to our forefathers, and to *remember* his holy covenant." The pious Jews who lived in the first century were, on the whole, a confused and dispirited lot. Having endured nearly 700 years as a despised minority with nationalistic longings under a succession of tyrannous regimes, there were many who believed that God had given up on his chosen ones. Perhaps some even thought that he had forgotten them. Even the most devout believer can have misgivings. The question "how long?" occurs in the Psalter nearly twenty times.

"How long?" How many times has that question passed our lips? As we waited for the surgeon's report. As we reached our wits' end with a rebellious teen or an unyielding parent. As we struggled to find the energy to finish an assignment. We must not be overly dramatic here, for most of us do not know the desolation of a race of people facing extermination. Nevertheless, it is possible to become so overwhelmed by the dire nature of our circumstances or to become so oppressed by a sense of hopelessness at the world's intractable problems that we fall into doubt, denial, and even despair.

The French existentialist philosopher Jean Paul Sartre was an atheist. But he found it distressing that God did not exist, because it left him stranded without a home or a goal to strive for. In striking words he lamented, "God is silent and that I cannot possibly deny—everything in me calls for God and that I cannot forget . . ."[3]

---

3. Quoted in Pinnock, *Reason Enough*, 41.

But into the dark pessimism of Sartre's existential angst, and into the circumstances that fray our own humanity, Zechariah breaks forth with luminous words,

> BLESSED be the Lord God of Israel;
> for he hath visited, and redeemed his people;
> And hath raised up a mighty salvation for us,
> in the house of his servant David.

This God, who had promised to Abraham and his descendants a destiny of plenty and freedom, untroubled by enemies and without fear, was about to make good on his oath. Though his people may have doubted, denied, and forgotten him, he has remembered them. This destiny has now drawn near in the appearance of the Baptist and, still more definitively, in the advent of the one whose coming it would be his task to proclaim.

My friends, whatever our lot in life, we must be convinced of this: God has remembered us. We may not be able to discern his mindfulness because that which assaults us confuses, distracts, and disorients. But we have tangible evidence of his memory that cannot elude us: the fellowship of his Church, the abiding Word of God, and perhaps most graphically the tokens of bread and wine. Are they not the very body and blood of him who is our "mighty salvation"? Do they not speak of God's personal intervention in time and space, to reconcile all things in himself? Do they not, by their very mundane and creaturely nature, demonstrate God's participation in the fabric of our world, working to bring order out of chaos and weaving our lives into the tapestry of his unfolding purpose?

St Luke has a word for this unfolding purpose: it is the word "salvation." If the first lesson we learn from the *Benedictus* is that we are a remembered people, the second is that God's re-membering of us is what is meant by "salvation." Luke has an interest in the theme of salvation that perhaps surpasses that of the other Gospel writers. He alone calls Jesus "Savior." And it is clear throughout his account of the life of Jesus that "salvation" includes deliverance, rescue, and victory. He heals a hemorrhaging woman, saying, "Your faith has *saved* you; go in peace" (7:50). He heals a blind man, saying, "Receive your sight; your faith has *saved* you" (18:42). To the penitently generous Zacchaeus he says, "Today *salvation* has come to this house" (19:9). All are examples of a re-membering, a repairing of the physical body or a bringing of health and renewal to a converted sinner.

But for St. Luke, salvation is even more profound than this. For it involves "the wholeness to which human beings are restored in a sound relation to God," to quote New Testament scholar Joseph Fitzmyer.[4] It is the embodiment of the prophet Isaiah's vision, which stood at the core of John's own proclamation:

> Every valley shall be exalted, and every mountain and hill shall be made low: and the crooked shall be made straight, and the rough places plain: And the glory of the LORD shall be revealed, and all flesh shall see it together (Luke 3:5–6; cf. Isa 40:4).

This is the ultimate re-membering. The plan of salvation is a restoration of what has been lost to us in the disordered pride of Eden and in every subsequent act of human will that divides us from ourselves, from one another, and from God. God's faithfulness to his word and covenant means that those who receive his offer of grace have an eternal place in the narrative of salvation he is writing.

---

4. Fitzmyer, *The Gospel According to Luke*, 222.

The Author of Salvation

In the medieval mind, God was conceived of as an Author, and it is from him that all authority is derived. His creative action began with the composition of the universe through his "word." "God said, 'Let there be light;' and there was light" (Gen 1:3). God spoke the cosmos into being through the power of his speech. The history of the world, therefore, was thought of as God laying out the events of human history as a novelist, penning characters and creating situations.[5] The tale he constructs is infinitely complex, with seemingly insignificant figures taking on major roles, while what is often regarded by us as greatness warrants merely a footnote.

Now, you and I are written into this story. From time to time we may be able to transcend our circumstances and get a sense of the movement of the divine plot. Every once in a while God will write a part for a prophet, assuring us that "through the tender mercy of our God" "the dayspring from on high hath visited us." But for the most part we are confused by the senseless succession of human affairs. What could possibly bring meaning out of our dismembered and dismembering experiences?

Every good Latinist knows that the proper rules of Latin grammar require the verb to come at the end of a sentence. In this epic we know as the human race, God has been piling up nouns and adjectives, particles and adverbs—each one waiting for its moment to become re-membered with the words around it through the introduction of the final verb—the *Verbum caro factum*—the "Word made flesh."

---

5. *Omnis mundi creatura / quasi liber et pictura / nobis est in speculum: / nostrae vitae, nostrae mortis, nostri status, nostrae sortis / fidele signaculum.* Alan of Lille, *De Miseria Mundi*, PL 210.579–80.

Let us take comfort from the fact that God has not forgotten us. He is working out his plan of salvation through the long-promised sending of his Son, whose coming has and will continue "to give light to them that sit in darkness, and in the shadow of death, / and to guide our feet into the way of peace."

The Song of Zechariah: Luke 1:68–79 (BCP1979)

68 Blessed be the Lord God of Israel;
 for he hath visited and redeemed his people;
69 And hath raised up a mighty salvation for us,
 in the house of his servant David;
70 As he spake by the mouth of his holy prophets,
 which have been since the world began:
71 That we should be saved from our enemies,
 and from the hands of all that hate us;
72 To perform the mercy promised to our forefathers,
 and to remember his holy covenant;
73 To perform the oath which he sware to our forefather Abraham,
 that he would grant us
74 That we being delivered out of the hands of our enemies
 might serve him without fear,
75 In holiness and righteousness before him,
 all the days of our life.

76 And thou, child, shalt be called the Prophet of the Highest:
 for thou shalt go before the face of the Lord to prepare his ways;

77 To give knowledge of salvation unto his people
   for the remission of their sins,
78 Through the tender mercy of our God,
   whereby the dayspring from on high hath visited us;
79 To give light to them that sit in darkness, and in the shadow of death,
   and to guide our feet into the way of peace.

8

Mary's Victorious Child: *Magnificat*

TERRY DONALDSON

MARY'S SONG OF PRAISE is one of the best known canticles. It is commonly referred to by the first word in its Latin version: *Magnificat anima mea dominum* (My soul magnifies the Lord). The song appears in the first chapter of Luke, in the scene where Mary has gone to visit Elizabeth. Elizabeth has just declared Mary to be blessed because she has been chosen by the Lord to give birth to the Messiah; the *Magnificat* is Mary's song of praise in response.

In his influential book *The Politics of Jesus*, John Howard Yoder says that, while we are not used to thinking of Mary as a social and political revolutionary, that is exactly what she sounds like in the *Magnificat*—someone who would have been quite at home among the ranks of the Maccabean rebels, celebrating one of their victories over the armies of their Hellenistic rulers. Indeed, the song is marked by a strikingly revolutionary and triumphal tone:

> [God has] "shown the strength of his arm; . . .
>
> he has cast down the mighty from their thrones
> and has lifted up the lowly;

> he has filled the hungry with good things and
> the rich he has sent away empty" (BAS).

Yoder goes on to say that at least we would be more able to hear this revolutionary tone "if it were not for the history of vain repetition in the liturgical use of the Magnificat."[1] As someone who has been greatly enriched by the forty years or so in which I have engaged in the liturgical repetition of the *Magnificat*, finding it anything but vain, I would like to think that Yoder was speaking a little tongue-in-cheek here. After all, he had a lot of friends and admirers from the more liturgical traditions. It might even be said in response that the revolutionary and triumphal tone of the *Magnificat* stands out even more sharply in the service of morning prayer, where the song is extracted from its scriptural context and is read or sung as a stand-alone text.

Be that as it may, here I will consider the *Magnificat* within its context in the Gospel of Luke, thinking especially of its character as a hymn of triumph. In doing so, it is certainly not my intention to take the sharp revolutionary edge off the hymn. Nevertheless, there are some things worth thinking about that emerge when we read it as part of the story Luke wants to tell.

The Babe, the Liberator

The first thing to note is hinted at already in the concluding part of the song: "He has helped his servant Israel . . . according to the promise he made to our ancestors, to Abraham and to his descendants forever." Throughout the first two chapters of Luke's Gospel, both John and Jesus are

---

1. Yoder, *The Politics of Jesus*, 26.

introduced in terms that are very much in keeping with traditional Jewish expectations about the Messiah and the restoration of Israel. The angel Gabriel announces to Mary that "the Lord God will give to [Jesus] the throne of his ancestor David; he will reign over the house of Jacob forever" (1:33). Zechariah sees in the birth of his son John a sign that God will "raise up a mighty [horn of] salvation for us in the house of his servant David," someone who will rescue us "from the hands of our enemies so that we might serve God without fear" (1:69, 74). After the birth of Jesus, Simeon is introduced as one who is "looking forward to the consolation of Israel" (2:25); likewise, Anna is "looking for the redemption of Jerusalem" (2:36–38). Luke begins his story of Jesus within the world of humble, pious, faithful Jews, all of them living "blamelessly according to all the commandments and regulations of the Lord" and waiting expectantly for the liberation of Jerusalem and the restoration of Israel.

A reader who comes to Luke without any knowledge of the Christian story would expect at this point that the story to follow would be one in which faithful Israel is delivered from its situation of oppression and suffering by the mighty victory that God accomplishes through the Messiah, thus bringing the promises made through the prophets to fulfilment. Mary's triumphal hymn differs from this straightforward story of suffering, victory, and fulfilment only in her use of the past tense: God has *already* cast down the mighty and lifted up the lowly; God has *already* come to Israel's aid in fulfilment of the promise. Evidently for Mary the miraculous conception of the Messiah in the past is enough in itself to guarantee that the deliverance of Israel is an imminent certainty.

We, however, are not innocent first-time readers; we know much more than Mary or Elizabeth do about how the story unfolds from here. Yes, we know that the story will involve suffering, victory, and fulfilment; but we also know that it will be much more complicated than a simple story of how the people of Israel are delivered from "their enemies and from the hand of all who hate them" by the mighty victory that God accomplishes through the Messiah. And so we cannot help but read the account of Mary's visit to Elizabeth with a certain element of anxious irony. Mary does not yet know that the one who Gabriel said would sit on the throne of his father David would be an itinerant preacher with nowhere to lay his head. Mary does not yet know that her son would die with the powerful still on their thrones and the humble still in a state of oppression. Mary is unaware that the announcement of Jesus as the King of the Judeans would come in the form of a mocking notice attached to his cross by a representative of the world's most powerful ruler. What would she have thought about her hymn of triumph at these points in the story? Would she have been inclined to ask, with John the Baptist, "Are you the one who was to come, or should we expect someone else?" Or would she have shared the disappointment of the disciples on the road to Emmaus: "We had hoped that he would be the one to redeem Israel"—the implication being that Jesus obviously couldn't have been; this is not the way the story of the Messiah is meant to end. But we also know that this is not the end of the story. God does show strength with his arm—by raising Jesus from the dead. There is a mighty victory, this time over death itself. And it turns out that this is how the promises are being fulfilled, through the life, death, and resurrection of the Messiah. But it is not the story that readers thought they were in for at the outset. The suffering of Israel as a people is a suffering that is also borne by the Messiah. The subjugation of the poor and hungry at the hands of the rich and powerful is also the experience of the Messiah himself. As Jesus himself says at the end of the Gospel: "Was it not necessary that the Messiah should suffer these things and [only] then enter into his glory?" (Luke 24:26). By the end of the Gospel, then, we are in a position to see that, while the story is one of suffering, victory, and fulfilment, the victory is won in an unexpected way, and the fulfilment is of a kind in which the promises are enlarged and reshaped even as they are being fulfilled. By the end of the Gospel we are also in a position to see that, in a real sense, the *Magnificat* can be understood as the story of Jesus from beginning to end: Jesus as the humble one who joins with the faithful poor of Israel in their suffering, even to the point of death, but is raised in a mighty show of divine strength, thus defeating the powers of sin and death, and preparing the way for that grand reversal that will set all things right.

The Ultimate Victory to Come

But we cannot end here. Even if we keep the whole story of Jesus in view as we repeat the *Magnificat* in our regular worship, we are nevertheless all too aware that we continue to live in a world where the powerful still seem to be sitting comfortably on their thrones, where the rich seem to be getting richer at the expense of the lowly, where the poor are going hungry in a world of plenty, and where the fulfilment of the promise made to Abraham and all his descendants seems to be receding ever further into the horizon.

Here I suggest that we can find a measure of hope and confidence in Mary's use of the past tense. Mary proclaims her hymn of triumph at a point in between the conception of the Messiah and the victory of the resurrection. The display of God's power in the conception of the Messiah gives her such confidence in the ultimate victory that she can speak about it in the past tense: God *has* "brought down the powerful from their thrones and lifted up the lowly." While we are at a different point in the story, we too are located between a mighty act of God in the past and the expectation of fulfilment in the future. We live in between the "Christ is risen" and the "Christ will come again." We may not want to follow Mary's example and put it all into the past tense; the intervening history between her day and ours leads us to be more cautious. Nevertheless, we have every reason to share her confidence; the resurrection of Christ gives us full confidence that the restoration of all things is assured. *Magnificemus dominum*: Let us magnify the Lord.

The Song of Mary: Luke 1:46–55 (International Consultation on English Texts)

46 My soul proclaims the greatness of the Lord,
47 my spirit rejoices in God my Savior;
    for he has looked with favor on his lowly servant.
From this day all generations will call me blessed:
    49 the Almighty has done great things for me,
    and holy is his name.
50 He has mercy on those who fear him
    in every generation.
51 He has shown the strength of his arm,
    he has scattered the proud in their conceit.

52 He has cast down the mighty from their thrones,
   and has lifted up the lowly.
53 He has filled the hungry with good things,
   and the rich he has sent away empty.
54 He has come to the help of his servant Israel,
   for he has remembered his promise of mercy,
55 The promise he made to our fathers,
   to Abraham and his children for ever.

9

Waiting for Salvation: *Nunc Dimittis*

Alan L. Hayes

THE GOSPEL OF LUKE introduces us to Jesus by evoking the faith and hope of first-century Judaism. In the first two chapters, three Jews bless the God of Israel in three prophetic and poetic proclamations that we call songs. The Song of Zechariah gives blessing to the God of Israel, whose covenant is one of mercy and salvation. The Song of Mary echoes the song of Hannah in 1 Samuel; like Hannah, Mary rejoices in a God who lifts the poor and judges the mighty. And the Song of Simeon brims with joy in the fulfilment of God's promises. All three of these songs in the Gospel of Luke reflect the poetry and prophecy of the Old Testament in their structure, references, and ethos.

We might say: what an odd thing! Luke seems to be the most gentile of the evangelists. And yet from the beginning of his gospel, here he is, putting us on notice that to know Jesus, we need to enter into the heart of Judaism. We need to resonate with the hope of Israel. One might almost imagine the marketing department at Luke's publishing house expostulating with him: "Are you sure you want to begin in such a Jewish way? It's likely to put off a lot of your readers! The Jews aren't that popular a group of people, you know. You'll be competing with the gospel of Thomas, which people can enjoy without being Jewish!"

But Luke wants us to *meet* Jesus, and that means meeting him in all his particularity as a first-century Jew. After all, we can't truly know anyone in abstraction from their cultural background and outlook. We can't know anyone if we think of them as a stereotype or a symbol or a metaphor or a personification of certain principles. Not only that—another reason for bringing us into the faith of Israel is that Luke wants us to realize from the beginning of his gospel that the world of the New Testament is in fact just the world of the Old Testament. The New Testament is not to be a corrective to the Old Testament, as some have thought, but its fulfilment. Remember how the Thirty-nine Articles of Religion of the Church of England puts it: "The Old Testament is not contrary to the New: for both in the Old and New Testament everlasting life is offered to Mankind by Christ."

Seeing the Messiah

Simeon sings out his song when the baby Jesus is presented at the Temple for what's called the redemption of the firstborn. In the liturgical calendar, Christians continue to commemorate this event in the Feast of the Presentation, which we call Candlemas, forty days after Christmas. The Song of Simeon is a central part of our liturgical celebration on Candlemas. In a way, it completes the Christmas story.

Luke tells us that, when the baby Jesus' parents presented him at the Temple, Simeon was an old man who had been waiting with longing and expectation for the coming of the Messiah, and for the consolation of Israel. Why did Israel need to be consoled? The way this question was answered by the Jewish philosopher Martin Buber is that this was a time of "the eclipse of God." It's not that God was absent from Israel, for there are no such times, but it was a time when the people's view of God and connection with God was obstructed. The three great institutions that had been established to keep God and Israel connected were no longer working. The kingship of Judea was held by an impostor appointed by the Roman government. The high priesthood was held by aristocrats who were also appointed by Rome. The king and the high priests alike were suspected by the people of not being really Jewish, of being instruments of oppression who were rewarded handsomely for their collaboration with the Roman Empire. And as for the third great institution of Old Testament Israel, prophecy, the line of prophets had come to an end. In fact, during the Maccabean revolt a couple of centuries earlier, some religious decisions had been deferred until such time as a true prophet should emerge. And people were still waiting.

So Simeon was waiting for the eclipse of God to be ended, and for the glory of God once more to shine in Israel, and this depended on God to fulfil his promise to send a real king, a real high priest, and a true prophet. Simeon was waiting for the Messiah, who would bring together all three of these offices. Simeon had received the promise from God that this Messiah would come before Simeon's death. When Luke talks of the consolation that Simeon expected, he uses the word that John uses for the Holy Spirit, the paraclete. So Simeon was waiting for the paracleting of Israel: that is, waiting for king, high priest, prophet, and Messiah to open Israel to the renewal of the Holy Spirit.

That day in Jerusalem, Simeon was directed by the Spirit to go to the Temple, and in that large crowd in that large space, somehow he recognized this particular couple and their baby coming from Bethlehem. I know something of how that feels. When my wife and I adopted our first child from the maternity ward at Peel General Hospital, we entered a room that was full of babies that we had never seen, but we both immediately knew which one was ours. And immediately Simeon, waiting at the Temple, somehow recognized this particular couple and this particular baby. He was now free to die with a peaceful and satisfied spirit. And today this Song of Simeon is often used at funerals, because it's a blessing to feel free to depart in the peace and satisfaction of knowing that God has redeemed us. "Lord, now you are letting your servant depart in peace, according to your word."

Salvation is Come

When Jesus' parents heard Simeon sing out in this way, they were amazed. We should be amazed as well. This little baby is the fulfilment of God's promise of salvation. And this is salvation on a large scale. It isn't personal salvation or even national salvation. It's salvation, Simeon says, that's prepared before the face of all peoples, and that brings God's revelation to the Gentiles. Spiritually speaking, this is a world-historical moment. On this morning in the Temple the faith of Israel is vindicated before the world, and the history of Israel begins to command the attention of all the nations.

And with this, God comes out of eclipse. God's light breaks through the walls of Israel's religious institutions, as it breaks through ours. Israel, first of all, reflects the glory of God; then the gentiles begin to come to the brightness of God's shining. And so the Song of Simeon reminds us of a song of Isaiah: 'Then your light shall break forth like the dawn, and your healing shall spring up quickly; your vindicator shall go before you; the glory of the LORD shall be your rear guard. And he shall startle many nations; kings shall shut their mouths because of him; for that which had not been told them they shall see.'

Simeon didn't live to see all of that played out, and neither shall we, but we can depart in peace knowing that the promise has already been fulfilled, and that we haven't missed the central fact of human history, which is what gives our lives their meaning.

The Song of Simeon: Luke 2:29–32 (English Standard Version)

29 Lord, now you are letting your servant depart in peace,
   according to your word;
30 for my eyes have seen your salvation
   that you have prepared in the presence of all peoples,
32 a light for revelation to the Gentiles,
   and for glory to your people Israel.

10

Being Like Christ: A Hymn to Christ

L. Ann Jervis

In the early years of the second century of the common era, a Roman official in Asia Minor named Pliny wrote to the emperor Trajan about the increasing problem of worshippers of Jesus Christ. Pliny described to Trajan some of the strange practices of these worshippers, among which was the singing of a hymn to Christ as if he were a god. A hymn to Christ—*carmen Christi* in Latin.

A hymn to Christ is what we find in Paul's letter to the Philippians. It may not be the hymn that Pliny reported the Christians in Asia Minor sang, but it is certainly an example of a hymn of Christ as if he were a god. Paul includes the hymn immediately after writing these words: "Do nothing from selfishness or conceit, but in humility count others better than yourselves. Let each of you look not only to your own interests but also to the interests of others."

Rooted in Christ's Character

I have a dear friend who has been my friend since we were fourteen. She, more than anyone I know, exemplifies the traits of unselfishness and humble service. She grew up in the same kind of Christian faith as I did—a kind of Christianity that emphasized doing good to others and de-emphasized meditating on, thinking about, or talking about the living convictions of the Christian faith which make self-sacrifice a fitting "modus operandi." It was a kind of Christianity that might occasionally glance at the Bible and theology when it momentarily took its focus off doing good. In the form of Christianity in which my friend and I were raised, there was lots of ethics but not very much theology.

Not surprisingly, my friend eventually let go of her Christian faith—it seemed unnecessary to her. She could do good for others and serve the poor without it. In my late teens I, on the other hand, found my way to a richer, thicker, and much more textured representation of the Christian faith than what my church had offered me. One of the gifts I found waiting for me was the Bible and the wealth of Christian thinking based on the Bible. In my case, this has not transformed me into a person who is nearly as unselfish and other-centred as my friend—that is a mystery I have no answer to. But it has offered me endless joy and resources I can't imagine living without.

As you might imagine, I have attempted to draw my friend towards the same discovery. But, as we all know, the mystery of faith is that it is a gift; and I, for one, am not the giver of that gift. But I have often wondered how or whether it might help my friend to consciously root her life of humble service to the poor in words of life such as this hymn to Christ. Of course, I don't know. I do know that I cannot do without this song, just as I can't do without the rest of Scripture.

This hymn in particular has given me hours and hours of satisfactory head-scratching—of pondering, of wondering, of imagining. I think that that is how Paul wanted the hymn to function. Like a piece of poetry that pierces our beings because it attempts to pierce mysteries.

Listening to the Expansive Horizons of God

There is space to share only some of the wonders I have found in this hymn. I'll focus primarily on the first stanzas: Have this disposition among you, which is also in Christ Jesus, who being in the form of God did not regard equality with God something to grasp after, but poured himself out, taking the form of a servant, being born in the likeness of humanity. And being found in human form he humbled himself, becoming obedient unto death.

These words stir questions like "What does it mean for Christ to be in the form of God—does this mean that Christ was really God, sort of God, or just looks like God?" Reading further, does the stanza about Christ not regarding equality with God something to grasp after mean that he wasn't equal to God or that he was? And what does the word *ekenosen*—which I have translated as "poured out," but which is often translated as "emptied"—mean? Does it mean that if Christ were God, Christ poured out his Godness in order to take on the form of a servant, being born in the likeness of humanity—that Christ needed to empty himself of his divinity in order to be born as a human?

The questions that stir from pondering this song are truly opportunities. They are chances to think deep down, to contemplate God's revelation in Christ Jesus.

The answers we come up with may not be as critical as the activity of contemplating. For as we contemplate we are opening ourselves to the expansive horizons of God. And as we do come up with answers, this hymn invites us not to stay satisfied and certainly not to close the book, as if now we know what the hymn is inviting us to sing. In that key, I offer my thoughts on some questions that the hymn stirs up.

Revealing Divinity in Humility

I hear Paul singing that Christ Jesus is in the form of God, in the very form of God. And that is why Paul goes on to sing that Christ's response to being equal to God is that he does not grasp at that equality. I hear Paul singing that Christ's divinity is characterized by not grasping at equality; Christ is God as Christ pours himself out and takes the form of a servant.

I hear Paul sing that Christ's divine character is such that he is God as he pours himself into human form. It is not that Christ empties himself of divinity in order to become human, but that Christ is divine in the very activity of being humble.

The song Paul sings extolls recognition of God as one who does not hold onto his divinity for himself alone. Paul sings about God as one whose divinity is defined by offering himself—offering himself through Christ. Paul's hymn proclaims that Christ's humility is the revelation of the true nature of divinity. And so I hear the hymn declaring that Christ's obedience is the revelation of the true way of being human. Obedient servanthood is the true nature of being human.

The song climaxes with soaring phrases that describe God, after Christ's obedience to death on a cross, lifting Christ up super high (*uperopsoosen*). This God does in order that at Jesus' name every knee might bow, whether in heaven or on earth or under the earth, and every tongue might confess that Jesus Christ is Lord for the sake of the glory of the Father.

God publicly and overwhelmingly affirms and endorses Christ's way of being divine—and Christ's way of being human. God's glory is found when all creation acknowledges the divinity and the humanity that Christ lives.

Becoming Human through Christ

There is so much more to ponder here, and consequently so much more depth and grounding on offer than what I could outline above. The hymn resonates with life-giving concepts that Paul clearly hopes will help the Philippians to have the disposition (*phronesis*) of Christ—what is often translated as the "mind" of Christ. The hymn reverberates with ideas meant to help people to be human the way Christ was human precisely because Christ's *divinity* is shaping them.

Singing this hymn could be instrumental in coming to have the character of Christ—the character of servants—recognizing that God is revealed as we are servants to each other, doing nothing from selfishness or conceit but looking out for the interests of others.

I know that I need to sing along with Paul, and so to ponder and wonder and ask questions over and over. In this way, to keep my heart and mind and soul and strength trained towards God's glory and not my own. I need to sing this hymn in order to open myself to sharing the disposition of Christ.

I wish my friend and many others—in fact, everybody—could hear this song. It might not make my friend into a better servant of the poor, but I believe that hearing this hymn in her heart would immensely enrich her life.

May we who have been blessed with being gifted with faith, and who have heard this hymn in our hearts, never stop singing this *carmen Christi*—this hymn to Christ. I believe that this is key to being in tune with God's work of transforming us and God's world. May we the church sing this hymn out—for it is God's song for God's world.

A Hymn to Christ: Philippians 2:5–11 (New Revised Standard Version)

5 Let the same mind be in you that was in Christ Jesus,
6 who, though he was in the form of God,
    did not regard equality with God
    as something to be exploited,
7 but emptied himself,
    taking the form of a slave,
    being born in human likeness.
And being found in human form,
    8 he humbled himself
    and became obedient to the point of death—
    even death on a cross.
9 Therefore God also highly exalted him
    and gave him the name
    that is above every name,

10 so that at the name of Jesus
every knee should bend,
in heaven and on earth and under the earth,
11 and every tongue should confess
that Jesus Christ is Lord,
to the glory of God the Father.

11

A Holy God: *Sanctus*

Judy Paulsen

As a freshly ordained church leader, about twenty years ago now, I attended a conference focused on the worship practices of the ancient church and their value for the twenty-first-century church. For many, especially those whose church follows some form of ancient liturgy, the value of ancient worship for today's church is obvious. But this conference was not aimed at so-called liturgical churches, and that is what interested me. It was held in a large Baptist church and was attended by about four hundred Baptist, Pentecostal, and Christian Reformed church leaders.

At one point during his address, the keynote speaker, Robert E. Webber, read aloud an ancient piece of liturgy. He read it slowly and powerfully. He then asked everyone to stand and read it aloud. And so together four hundred Baptist, Pentecostal, and Christian Reformed people, and me, the sole Anglican, said together:

> Holy, holy, holy Lord,
> God of power and might,
> Heaven and earth are full of your glory.

> Hosanna in the highest.
> Blessed is he who comes in the name
> of the Lord.
> Hosanna in the highest.

At the end you could have heard a pin drop. I said to myself, "Was that the *Sanctus*?" I felt both proud and ashamed. I was proud that this glorious ancient hymn was a part of my own Anglican tradition. But I was ashamed that I had for decades rattled those words off so flippantly. As so often has happened for me, it took someone originally from another tradition to help me appreciate the riches of my own Anglican way.

Song of Angels, Song of Humanity

In the Anglican Communion service, the *Sanctus*, referred to by the Latin for "holy," forms the last part of the Preface in the Prayer of Consecration, and is normally sung or said by the whole congregation. It is made up of two parts. The first part is from an acclamation found in Isaiah 6:3. The second part is from an acclamation found in Matthew 21:9 (which itself is an echo of Psalm 118:26).

The *Sanctus* brings these two parts together: a sort of "meeting place" of these Old and New Testament texts. It is one of the most ancient pieces of Christian liturgy, referred to in several ancient documents. St. Clement of Rome (who died at the start of the second century) already refers, in his letter to the Corinthian Church, to Isaiah 6:3 being sung in church. Other early church fathers also refer to it, including Tertullian, Athanasius, and John Chrysostom. And since at least the start of the fifth century, the *Sanctus* has been part of the Western Church's Eucharistic rite.

Leaning into God's Holiness

But what does the *Sanctus* offer us besides a firm rooting in these two acclamations from Scripture and in early Christian tradition? The *Sanctus* has a particular gift to offer the Church in our age. It is a gift of correction—correction for a theology, and so preaching and teaching, that so often leans into the love of God, but much more rarely into the holiness, power, and might of God. And the sort of *love* we so often lean into is a love that is palatable to the broader culture—basically, abiding affection.

It is firstly, a sort of *insipid* affection. One that is blind to wrongdoing and says "There, there. You're just not yourself today." It is as if the self was truly the locus of proper judgement. In this framework we humans are made out to be the *rightful* eaters of the fruit of the knowledge of good and evil.

Secondly this culturally palatable love is a sort of *impotent* affection. It is a love that cannot really *do much*, but sits there handwringing over the way we treat each other and treat the rest of creation. Always hoping for the best, but never able to do anything about it.

This is "God's love" made palatable to a society that has placed the Self as Lord. And it is to this the *Sanctus* offers a much needed corrective. With its thrice repeated "Holy, holy, holy Lord," the *Sanctus* points to God as the one true measure of holiness, and the proper locus of judgement: the triune God, Father, Son, and Holy Spirit, who is also our rightful Lord.

The wise old New Testament scholar William Barclay writes,

> The basic idea of holiness is difference. God is different from us. Precisely there is the reason that we are moved to adoration. The very

> mystery of God moves us to awed admiration in his presence and to amazed love that that greatness should stoop so low for us and our salvation.[1]

For Barclay, the "difference"—the holiness—is not some abstract essence existing in distant transcendence. Rather, God's holiness is self-revealed in his relation to us humans.

As former Wycliffe professor of theology John Webster has written in a little book simply entitled *Holiness*:

> Talk of God's holiness indicates the manner in which the sovereign God relates. As the Holy One, God passes judgement on sin and negates it. Yet the holy God does this, not from afar, as a detached legislator, but in the reconciling mission of the Son and the outpouring of the sanctifying Spirit.[2]

He is the Triune Living God who is "holy, holy, holy," and by his own being and actions is rightful Lord.

The *Sanctus* continues with an assertion of the omnipotence of God: "God of power and might." This power and might is seen in God's own self-revelatory acts. He is the creator of reality itself—commanding the winds and waves, healing the leper, forgiving the sinner, providing for the hungry, raising the dead. God's is a power and might revealed in that "for our sake he made him who knew no sin to be sin for us, so that in him we might become the righteousness of God" (2 Cor 5:21). It is a power and might revealed in the continuing sanctifying work of the Spirit. It is so clear that *this* power and might are unlike any we ourselves define. It is the power and might of the Triune

---

1. Barclay, *The Revelation of John*, 162.
2. Webster, *Holiness*, 47.

Living God whose glory fills heaven and earth, as Isaiah 6:3 so succinctly points out.

The second part of the *Sanctus*, based on Matthew 21:9, echoes the shout of praise and adoration made in recognition of the messiahship of Jesus, as he entered Jerusalem riding on a simple donkey. Hosanna, with its literal meaning "recues" or "saves," again points to God himself. And it is Jesus, whose name literally means "God saves," who comes in the name of (in the authority and power of) the Lord God.

Worship of the Triune God

This then is the full and rich teaching of the *Sanctus*: the holiness, the power and might, the saving provision of God. May we allow this teaching to shape us, to prepare us to offer worship—not to some pale impotent god of our own making, but to the Triune Living God himself, who alone is worthy of praise and adoration.

Sanctus: Isaiah 6:3, Matthew 21:9 (International Consultation on English Texts)

Holy, holy, holy Lord,
God of power and might,
Heaven and earth are full of your glory.
    Hosanna in the highest.

Blessed is he who comes in the name of the Lord.
    Hosanna in the highest.

12

Sing, Church: *Dignus es*

Joseph L. Mangina

The book of Revelation is known for many things: its mysterious symbols, its grotesque imagery, its bizarre cast of characters—a dragon, a beast, locust warriors, a woman clothed with the sun—as well its dark and dualistic view of a rebellious world standing under the judgment of God. Especially in our time it has become known for its supposed atmosphere of violence, no doubt reflecting the repressed resentment felt by a minority group that would like nothing better than to see the dominant society be cast into the lake of fire. If ever there was a biblical book that fit Jonathan Edwards's description "sinners in the hands of an angry God," this would be it! The Apocalypse is undoubtedly dualistic in its way—God versus the world, St. Michael versus Satan, the apocalyptic army of the 144,000 sealed versus the Beast whose number is 666. In a world suspicious of dualisms of all sorts, the Apocalypse does not come off looking very good. It is typical sectarian literature, and we, especially Anglicans, all know that sectarianism is a bad thing, right?

I do not intend to bury the Apocalypse, however, but to praise it. Or rather, to commend the Apocalypse for *its* praise of the Lord God of Israel, whom Christians worship as the Father, the Son, and the Holy Spirit. Before the Apocalypse is a book of judgment and vengeance, it is a radically *theocentric* book. Precisely because it is theocentric it is also liturgical and musical. It is really amazing to see just how much worship there is in the Apocalypse. Besides the passages combined in the canticle known as the *Song to the Lamb*, there is the song of the great multitude in chapter 7, the new song sung by the Lamb's army in chapter 14, and the song of Moses and the Lamb in chapter 15, and of course "Hallelujah! The Lord God omnipotent reigneth" in chapter 19, from which Handel drew his famous "Hallelujah Chorus" in—appropriately—his oratorio *Messiah*. If you do not understand the music of the Apocalypse, you will not understand its peculiar and powerful witness. Our concern here is with the first real liturgical bit, in chapter 4 and then in the passage from chapter 5, which are combined in the church's *Song to the Lamb*.

The Lamb and the Scroll

Chapter 4 opens with John being lifted up to heaven to behold the heavenly worship, the four living creatures, and the twenty-four elders forever singing before the throne of the Lord God almighty. That worship begins with the *Sanctus*, the seraphic cry of "Holy, Holy, Holy," which Judy Paulsen exposits in her meditation. It continues with the ascription of praise to God for his astonishing action as the Creator: "Worthy are you, our Lord and God, to receive glory and honor and power, for you created all things, and by your will they existed and were created" (Rev 4:11

ESV). The church and the synagogue share this conviction that nothing that is *has* to be; you and I exist only because God willed it. It is an astonishing thought.

Yet John's vision of heaven is not yet finished. "Then I saw in the right hand of him who was seated on the throne a scroll written within and on the back, sealed with seven seals" (Rev 5:1). Anton Chekhov famously said that if a gun appears in Act 1 of a play, it has to go off before the end of Act 5. The scroll is firmly sealed; it must be opened. But here's the thing, John's angel declares that the seal cannot be opened except by one who is worthy. On hearing this John weeps "loudly," for there is no one on heaven or on earth or under the earth who can open the scroll. You can read this passage many ways; but here is my take on it. The contents of the scroll are God's providential rule of history, the means by which he will bring creation to fulfilment and make things "come out right" in the end. But the scroll is sealed; there is no creature who can open it; and so the world remains a dark and puzzling place. If I had to assign a theological name to it, I would say the scroll sums up the question of theodicy, the question whether the God who is Justice itself is *actually* just, just in a way that matters for creatures like ourselves.

And that is why John weeps. There is nothing more human than weeping. As David wept over Absalom, and as the Psalmist wept through the night, and as Jesus wept over Jerusalem, and as Mary wept in the garden, so John weeps. The NRSV says he "wept bitterly," but that's pretty interpretive; the Greek just says *eklaion polu*—"he wept a lot." No doubt he did. There is a lot to weep for. This is not the place to offer a Christian reading of our political situation in this year of our Lord 2016, but I will say this one thing. Between Brexit, Trump's victory, the European refugee crisis, the horrors of Syria, and God knows what else, any notion that we have arrived at a bright new day of justice, peace, and global security has been exposed as hopelessly naive. History goes on; and while it does, there will be plenty of room for tears.

But in our passage, this note of lament is touched on only briefly; the main thrust is affirmative—we might say, evangelical. For it turns out there *is* one who is worthy to open the scroll, one who not only knows God's providential rule but is the very agent of that rule. Thus the angel announces that the Lion of Judah, the Root of David, has conquered; *therefore* he is worthy to open the scroll with its seven seals. The Lion of Judah, in a surprising twist, turns out to be a Lamb—not just a Lamb but a Lamb slaughtered and strangely alive, and not just a Lamb slaughtered but one endowed with seven horns and seven eyes, symbols of his messianic power and infinite knowledge, a Lamb filled with the Lord's own Spirit.

This Lamb, of course, is Jesus Christ. Jesus is not just the clue to our history, he is our history. He is the divine-human life that God is drawing us into. A lot of the imagery in Revelation is harsh, yes, and it surely stands in need of careful interpretation. But it is harsh because we humans do not easily yield control of our lives. The wrath of God is but the love of God turned against the violence and falsehood of this world. God is against us only because he is for us; truly against us in our sin, and truly for us as he has taken up our cause in the person of his Son, the Lion-Lamb who has won the victory on our behalf.

A People Who Sing

Our greatest fear, I think, is that God intends to bludgeon us into submission in the end. God wins; therefore creatures must lose. But that is not the Lord's way, his economy or his grace. No, what the Lord wants to do is *sing* us into submission. As soon as the Lamb takes the scroll from the hand of the Almighty, before he can even open it, the four living creatures and the twenty-four elders fall down before him and sing a "new song." It is a song of victory, praising the Crucified for his ransoming a *people* out of every tribe and language and people and nation of the earth. "Wow," we say, "how amazing"—God has called into being this incredible community, this perfect people, this invisible church. If only there were really a people like this. A people that knows when to weep, and when to sing. A people that knows not just what to sing for but whom to sing to. A people who live by worship of the Lord God almighty; a people who sing praises to the Lamb; a people whose tongues are loosed by the Holy Spirit of God. If only we could find such a people, we would be sure to join up in a minute!

It's too late, though. We are already that people. We, the visible and all too imperfect church. The elders' song and the living creatures' song and the angels' song is our song. The first time you stepped into a church and opened your mouth to sing, it was your song. From your mother's womb it was your song, the very music of your birth and baptism; you, Christian sisters and brothers, were summoned into existence just to sing this song. And once this song begins there is no end of it. By the time Revelation 5 is over, it is not just angels and elders and prophets and heavenly beings, and you and me, who are singing, but "every creature in heaven and on earth and under the earth and in the sea, and all that is in them, saying, 'To him who sits on the throne and to the Lamb be blessing and honor and glory and might forever and ever!'" The church from all nations, surrounded by a vast cosmic chorus of praise. What is the relation between music and mission? There is no relation; they are the same thing, when the music is *this* music, and the One to whom we sing it the Lord God Almighty. To sing is to be sent: this is what is called "missional ecclesiology."

"Worthy is the Lamb who was slain . . . To him who sits on the throne and to the Lamb be blessing and honor and glory and might forever and ever." The church is that people who have been given the freedom to sing this song, who cannot *not* sing it. So sing, Christian. Sing your heart out. Sing in the night of tears, and in the day of rejoicing. Don't worry if you can't carry a tune; the tune will carry you. And as you sing, you will find yourself in the company of saints and angels and elders and cosmic beings, and not least your fellow Christian. Let us sing as the church, and live as the church, and go on mission as the church, and be thankful. Amen.

A Song to the Lamb: Revelation 4:11; 5:9–10, 13 (BCP 1979)

4:11 Splendor and honor and kingly power
    are yours by right, O Lord our God,
For you created everything that is,
    and by your will they were created and have their being;

5:9 And yours by right, O Lamb that was slain,
    for with your blood you have redeemed for God,

From every family, language, people, and nation,
> 10 a kingdom of priests to serve our God on earth.

13 And so, to him who sits upon the throne,
> and to Christ the Lamb,

Be worship and praise, dominion and splendor,
> for ever and for evermore.

Bibliography

Alan of Lille. *De Miseria Mundi*. PL 210. Edited by J. P. Migne. Garnier: 1855.

Augustine. *Quaest. in Heptateuch*. PL 34. Edited by J. P. Migne. Paris: 1841.

Barclay, William. *The Revelation of John*. Volume 1. Louisville, KY: Westminster John Knox, 1976.

Baxter, M. Elizabeth. *The Women in the Word*. 2nd edition. London: Christian Herald, 1897.

Boethius, Anicius Manlius. *De Musica. The Fundamentals of Music*. Translated by Calvin M. Bower. Edited by Claude Palisca. Music Theory Translation Series. New Haven, CT: Yale University Press, 1989.

Book of Alternative Services of the Anglican Church of Canada. Toronto, ON: Anglican Book Centre, 1985.

Book of Common Prayer of the Anglican Church of Canada. Toronto, ON: Anglican Book Centre, 1962.

The Book Of Common Prayer and Administration of the Sacraments and Other Rites and Ceremonies of the Church: Together with the Psalter or Psalms of David According to the Use of the Episcopal Church. New York: Seabury Press, 1979.

Calvin, John. *Institutes of the Christian Religion*. Translated by Henry Beveridge. Grand Rapids: Eerdmans, 1995.

Coverdale, Miles. *Goostly Psalmes and Spirituall Songes*. In *Works of Miles Coverdale: Remains*. Edited by George Pearson. Cambridge: Parker Society, 1846.

BIBLIOGRAPHY

de Rothschild, Constance, and Annie de Rothschild. *The History and Literature of the Israelites, according to the Old Testament and the Apocrypha. Vol. I: The Historical Books.* 2nd edition. London: Longmans, 1871.

Fitzmyer, Joseph. *The Gospel According to Luke (I–IX).* Anchor Bible Commentary. New York: Doubleday, 1981.

Hooker, Richard. *Of the Laws of Ecclesiastical Polity: A Critical Edition.* Edited by Arthur Stephen McGrade. Oxford: Oxford University Press.

Lowth, Robert. *Lectures on the Sacred Poetry of the Hebrews.* Translated by G. Gregory. Edited by Calvin E. Stowe. Andover: Crocker & Brewster: 1829.

M. G. *Women Like Ourselves: Short Addresses for Mothers' Meetings, Bible Classes, etc.* London: SPCK, 1893.

Mercier, Anne. *The Story of Salvation: Thoughts on the Historical Study of Scripture.* London: Rivingtons, 1887.

Pinnock, Clark. *Reason Enough: a case for the Christian Faith.* Burlington: Welch, 1985.

Santmire, H. Paul. *The Travail of Nature: The Ambiguous Ecological Promise of Christian Theology.* Minneapolis: Fortress, 1985.

Schroeder, Joy. *Deborah's Daughters: Gender Politics and Biblical Interpretation.* Oxford: Oxford University Press.

Smith, Eliza. *The Battles of the Bible.* Edinburgh: Paton & Ritchies, 1852.

Spurgeon, Charles. Sermons. http://www.spurgeon.org/sermons/0763.php.

Stanton, Elizabeth Cady. "The Book of Judges, Chapter II." In *The Woman's Bible, Part II: Joshua to Revelation*, edited by Elizabeth Cady Stanton, 20–21. Boston: Northeastern University Press, 1898.

Stowe, Harriet Beecher. *Woman in Sacred History.* New York: Ford, Howard, & Hulbert, 1873.

Taylor, Marion Ann, and Christiana de Groot, eds. *Women of War Women of Woe: Joshua and Judges through the Eyes of Nineteenth-Century Female Biblical Interpreters.* Grand Rapids: Eerdmans, 2016.

Webster, John. *Holiness.* Grand Rapids: Eerdmans, 2003.

Woosnam, Etty. *The Women of the Bible: Old Testament.* 4th edition. London: Partridge, 1881.

Yoder, John Howard. *The Politics of Jesus.* Grand Rapids: Eerdmans, 1972.

List of Contributors

Stephen G. W. Andrews
Principal and Helliwell Professor of Biblical Interpretation

Annette Brownlee
Chaplain, Professor of Pastoral Theology, and Director of Field Education

Terence Donaldson
Lord and Lady Coggan Professor of New Testament Studies

Alan L. Hayes
Bishops Frederick and Heber Wilkinson Professor of Church History

L. Ann Jervis
Professor of New Testament

Joseph L. Mangina
Professor of Systematic Theology

Judy Paulsen
Professor of Evangelism, Director of the Institute of Evangelism

Thomas P. Power
Adjunct Professor of Church History, Theological Librarian

LIST OF CONTRIBUTORS

Ephraim Radner
Professor of Historical Theology

Peter Robinson
Professor of Proclamation, Worship, and Ministry

J. Glen Taylor
Professor of Scripture and Global Christianity

Marion Taylor
Professor of Old Testament

Katherine Kennedy Steiner teaches liturgy and music at Wycliffe College. Her research is on music and liturgy in the medieval church, for which she received a Mellon Fellowship at the Pontifical Institute of Mediaeval Studies in Toronto, working on her book project, *The Second City: Notre Dame Polyphony and English Liturgy at St Andrews Cathedral.*

www.ingramcontent.com/pod-product-compliance
Lightning Source LLC
Chambersburg PA
CBHW070512090426
42735CB00012B/2755